Studies in Logic
Volume 41

Symbolic Knowledge
from Leibniz to Husserl

Volume 30
Logic and Philosophy Today, Volume 2
Johan van Benthem and Amitabha Gupta, eds

Volume 31
Nonmonotonic Reasoning. Essays Celebrating its 30th Anniversary
Gerhard Brewka, Victor W. Marek and Miroslaw Truszczynski, eds.

Volume 32
Foundations of the Formal Sciences VII. Bringing together Philosophy and Sociology of Science
Karen François, Benedikt Löwe, Thomas Müller and Bart van Kerkhove, eds.

Volume 33
Conductive Argument. An Overlooked Type of Defeasible Reasoning
J. Anthony Blair and Ralph H. Johnson, eds.

Volume 34
Set Theory
Kenneth Kunen

Volume 35
Logic is not Mathematical
Hartley Slater

Volume 36
Understanding Vagueness. Logical, Philosophical and Linguistic Perspectives
Petr Cintula, Christian G. Fermüller, Lluís Godo and Petr Hájek, eds.

Volume 37
Handbook of Mathematical Fuzzy Logic. Volume 1
Petr Cintula, Petr Hájek and Carles Noguera, eds.

Volume 38
Handbook of Mathematical Fuzzy Logic. Volume 2
Petr Cintula, Petr Hájek and Carles Noguera, eds.

Volume 39
Non-contradiction
Lawrence H. Powers, with a Foreword by Hans V. Hansen

Volume 40
The Lambda Calculus. Its Syntax and Semantics
Henk P. Barendregt

Volume 41
Symbolic Knowledge from Leibniz to Husserl
Abel Lassalle Casanave, ed.

Studies in Logic Series Editor
Dov Gabbay   dov.gabbay@kcl.ac.uk

Symbolic Knowledge from Leibniz to Husserl

Edited by
Abel Lassalle Casanave

© Individual author and College Publications 2012.
All rights reserved.

ISBN 978-1-84890-073-8

College Publications
Scientific Director: Dov Gabbay
Managing Director: Jane Spurr
Department of Informatics
King's College London, Strand, London WC2R 2LS, UK

http://www.collegepublications.co.uk

Original cover design by Orchid Creative   www.orchidcreative.co.uk
Printed by Lightning Source, Milton Keynes, UK

All rights reserved. No part of this publication may be reproduced, stored in a retrieval system or transmitted in any form, or by any means, electronic, mechanical, photocopying, recording or otherwise without prior permission, in writing, from the publisher.

Table of Contents

Contributing Authors   vii

Preface   ix

Representing and Abstracting
An Analysis of Leibniz's Concept of Symbolic Knowledge   1

   OSCAR M. ESQUISABEL

Kant's Avatars of Symbolic Knowledge
The Role of Symbolic Manipulation in Kant's Philosophy of Mathematics   51

   ABEL LASSALLE CASANAVE

Between Calculus and Semantic Analysis
Symbolic Knowledge in the Origins of Mathematical Logic   79

   JAVIER LEGRIS

Away from the Facts
Symbolic Knowledge in Husserl's Philosophy of Mathematics   115

   JAIRO JOSÉ DA SILVA

Contributing Authors

Abel LASSALLE CASANAVE
UFBA / CNPq (Brazil)

Professor of Philosophy, Faculty of Philosophy and Human Sciences, Federal University of Salvador (UFBA), and Researcher at the National Council for Scientific and Technological Development (CNPq), Brazil
e-mail: abel.lassalle@gmail.com

Oscar M. ESQUISABEL
UNQ – UNLP / CONICET (Argentina)

Professor of Metaphysics, Faculty of Humanities and Educational Sciences, National University of La Plata, and Researcher at the National Council of Scientific Research (CONICET), Argentina.
e-mail: omesqui1@speedy.com.ar

Javier LEGRIS
UBA / CEF-CONICET (Argentina)

Professor of Logic, School of Economics, University of Buenos Aires, and Researcher at the National Council of Scientific Research (CONICET), Argentina.
e-mail: jlegris@retina.ar

Jairo José da SILVA
UNESP-RIO CLARO / CNPq (Brazil)

Professor of Mathematics (retired), São Paulo State University, and Senior Researcher, National Council for Scientific and Technological Development (CNPq), Brazil.
e-mail: dasilvajairo1@gmail.com

Preface

Symbolic Knowledge from Leibniz to Husserl

Intuitive knowledge, Leibniz tells us, is knowledge obtained by considering directly ideas that have been completely analyzed into their simplest components that are *per se nota*, that is, also intuitively known. *Symbolic*, he proceeds, is the knowledge obtained by means of *characters*, i.e. *signs* that can present themselves in many different formats, written, carved, drawn, etc. Mathematical symbols, typically, but also musical or stenographic signs, the symbols of chemistry, words of natural language, geometrical figures and many other graphic signs. However, it is arithmetic and algebra that provide the paradigmatic instances of symbolic knowledge. Indeed, the manipulation of arithmetical and algebraic symbols according to rules – i.e. the operations of a *calculus* – does not require intuitive knowledge, which is why symbolic knowledge is also often called *blind* knowledge.

More precisely, thinking carried out or knowledge obtained with the help of the characters of natural language – the words – can be better characterized as *verbal* thinking or knowledge. Verbal knowledge is not fit for a calculus, nor can be done without considering the corresponding ideas. Other semiotic systems, such as diagrams (geometric or not), maps, tables, etc. occupy an intermediate position between the verbal and the symbolic; knowledge provided by them could be called, for lack of better words, *graphic* knowledge.

Our book considers only symbolic knowledge *strictu sensu*, whose model is algebra. But graphic knowledge (to a lesser extent) and verbal knowledge (to a larger extent) are also objects of attention – if only to provide an opportune contrast with symbolic knowledge proper. Indeed, the cognitive advantages of symbolic knowledge, which depends on the willingness of artificial languages to be implemented as *calculi*, are systematically contrasted with the shortcomings usually attributed to natural languages and other graphic methods.

From Leibniz, through Kant, Frege and the "Booleans" to Husserl, the chapters are offered as contributions to the conceptual understanding of symbolic knowledge and the uses it can be put to. Symbolic knowledge is, as already mentioned, a *calculus*, which can – to name a few of its uses – help to render thinking *sensory*, afford intellectual *economy*, and play a relevant *heuristic* role.

Other traditional problems of logic, philosophy of formal sciences, epistemology, philosophy of language and even metaphysics and philosophical methodology are also dealt with in the chapters; among them, questions concerning content and form, signs and representation, structural knowledge and isomorphism, language and calculus, and real and ideal elements.

In the first chapter, entitled "Representing and Abstracting. An Analysis of Leibniz's Concept of Symbolic Knowledge", Oscar Miguel Esquisabel carefully discriminates among many different functions symbolic systems can have, according to Leibniz (some have just been mentioned above) – distinctions to which the other authors have, in different degrees, remained faithful. Having them in mind, Esquisabel shows that Leibniz had two different projects concerning symbolic knowledge. One is that known as *Ars Characteristica Universalis*, a *lingua universalis* in which characters surrogate concepts of a no less universal Encyclopedia, which however serves not only as a means of communication, but also as a *calculus ratiocinator*. Another is that of a science of *Forms*, which still takes the form of a calculus, but only in the sense of manipulations according to rules of signs that no longer stand for any particular concepts or entities.

In the following chapter, "Kant's Avatars of Symbolic Knowledge. The Role of Symbolic Manipulation in Kant's Philosophy of Mathematics", Abel Lassalle Casanave distinguishes three kinds of symbolic knowledge: as a substitute for intuitive knowledge; as an instrumental extension of intuitive knowledge; and as formal knowledge of relations. They are seen as different ways of dealing with the problems resulting from the "algebraic way of thinking", which came to light in the 17th century. Lassalle Casanave's strategy of argumentation consists in detecting different types of symbolic knowledge in Kant's philosophy – from the possibility of symbolic knowledge as formal knowledge in the pre-critique period to its role as a substitute of intuitive knowledge in the *Critique of Pure Reason* – by means of a systematic analysis of the already mentioned functions signs can have in symbolic systems.

In "Between Calculus and Semantic Analysis. Symbolic Knowledge in the Origins of Mathematical Logic", Javier Legris puts the concept of symbolic knowledge to work for a better understanding of the origins of symbolic logic. Although it has already been noticed that the distinction between language and calculus can sustain two alternative foundational programs for logic, associated respectively with the works of Frege and the Booleans, Legris reminds us that the distinction between *lingua universalis* and *calculus ratiocinator* is an epistemological one. This allows him to distinguish between Frege and the Booleans, associating the latter with the epistemological tradition of symbolic knowledge and the former with his own semantic revolution. In so doing, Legris contrasts the eminently epistemological problem concerning the access to objects with the semantic problem concerning the *reference* to objects, and the type of knowledge associated with it, that underlies the formalization of the so-called "contents of judgment".

In the last chapter of this book, "Away from the Facts. Symbolic Knowledge in Husserl's Philosophy of Mathematics", Jairo José da Silva shows that the problem of symbolic knowledge runs through the entire corpus of Husserl's philosophy, and that following this tread can help us to understand his philosophical development, in particular during the last decade of the 19th century, when phenomenology was born. Da Silva shows that whereas Husserl's approach to the problem posed by symbolic knowledge involving surrogating symbols is fairly standard – in this case, he thinks, symbolic manipulations mirror intuitive operations – in the case of non-interpreted symbols, which are, at best, taken as standing for purely "imaginary" entities, Husserl's treatment is more nuanced. Although Husserl believed, according to da Silva, that in both cases some sort of knowledge is obtained, he restricted, for epistemological reasons, the applicability of symbolic reasoning involving "imaginaries" in material sciences, whereas giving it free rein in formal sciences, like formal mathematics.

A last word concerning the unity of the book is in order. There is indeed a unity here, not only of theme, but also of concepts and perspectives, born out of the joint participation of the authors in many seminars, short courses and round tables, in Brazil, Argentine and Uruguay, and, in particular, the annual meetings of the Southern Cone Colloquia on the Philosophy of Formal Sciences (held at the Federal University of Santa Maria, in the Brazilian state of Rio Grande do Sul). In fact, this book contains only the first part of a continuing project, which will be completed with the publication, shortly, we expect, of another book, planned to be called "Symbolic Knowledge from Wolff to Weyl".

We take this opportunity to thank the many colleagues and students who contributed with their valuable comments and suggestions. Finally, the authors want to dedicate this book to Oswaldo Chateaubriand, on the occasion of his retirement, as a token of our friendship.

The Authors
Montevideo, Fall of 2012

1

Representing and abstracting

An Analysis of Leibniz's Concept of Symbolic Knowledge[*]

OSCAR M. ESQUISABEL

The use of the concept of symbolic knowledge (*cognitio symbolica*, *symbolische Erkenntnis*) is widespread in German post-Leibnizian thought. We can find it in the works of Wolff, Baumgarten, Daries and Lambert, even in Kant's pre-critical works, and in post-Kantian philosophers such as Salomon Maimon.[1] In a general way, it was applied to all knowledge for which some kind of symbolic mediation was required. Even for the philosophers who were in one way or another under the influence of Leibnizian thought, the symbolic knowledge notion was closely tied to the possibility of constructing symbolic languages and logical calculi in order to formalize conceptual relations and inferential operations.

The term was coined by Leibniz, and its later reception depended in great measure on the essay *Meditationes de cognitione, veritate et ideiis*[2] that Leibniz published for the first time in the *Acta Eruditorum*, November 1684

---

[*] The content of this paper was presented, discussed, and developed in the frame of many workshops, conferences and courses in Argentina, Brasil and Germany. I would like to mention especially the Workshop on Mathematical Epistemology (Bielefeld, 2003), where I lectured a first draft of the paper, and the Colóquios Conesul de Filosofia das Ciências Formais (UFSM, Brasil), which offered to me repeatedly the opportunity to clarify and to improve my points of view. And above all, I would wish to thank the invaluable stimuli that were for me the work, ideas and suggestions of Prof. Dr. Abel Lassalle Casanave (UFBA, Brasil), Prof. Dr. Javier Legris (UBA, Argentina), Prof. Dr. Volker Peckhaus (Universität Paderborn, Germany), and Prof. Dr. Jairo José da Silva (UNESP, Brasil). This work was supported by the Deutscher Akademischer Austausch Dienst (DAAD, Germany); the Fundación Antorchas (Argentina); the Consejo Nacional de Investigaciones Científicas y Técnicas (CONICET, Argentina); the Universidad Nacional de La Plata (UNLP, Argentina) and the Agencia para la Promoción de la Ciencia y la Tecnología (ANPCyT, Argentina).
[1] Wolff, Chr., *Psychologia Empirica*, § 287 et ss, p 205 et ss.; Baumgarten, A. G., *Metaphysica*, § 620 et ss, p 226 et ss. Cfr. Schweiger (2001), 1178-1183. Daries, *Introductio in Artem inveniendi*, § 99 et ss, p 79 et ss; Lambert, J. H., *Neues Organon, Semiotik*, 5-43; Maimon, S., *Versuch über die transzendentalphilosophie*, p 263-333. For Kant, see Ch. 2.
[2] A VI 4, 585. From now on quoted as *Meditationes*.

(and that was reissued again in 1740, after Leibniz's death). Nevertheless, when we try to examine more carefully the notion of symbolic knowledge *qua leibnizian concept*, there is something that can produce some perplexity: the occurrences of the expression "symbolic knowledge" are extremely rare in the writings of the philosopher from Leipzig.

If we take the more important works of his mature period, between *Meditationes* (or perhaps a little before) and the *Nouveaux Essais* (1703-1704), the expression "symbolic knowledge" appears only once in *Meditations* and "symbolic thought" twice in the same essay.[3] But it is difficult to find any other occurrence of terms such as "symbolic knowledge" or "symbolic thought" in other writings of the same period. If we consider epistemic concepts such as "notion" and "concept", which are correlated with "knowledge" and "thought", one cannot find a single instance of the combination "symbolic notion" or "symbolic concept".

Thus, textual analysis reveals to us that before and after the *Meditationes* Leibniz preferred to use other expressions with the same (or approximately the same) conceptual content as what he called "symbolic knowledge" or "symbolic thought" in *Meditationes*. Contrary to what happens with both terms, these other denominations appear many times and can been traced back to the first publications of the young Leibniz with remarkable recurrence and constancy. Such denominations are "blind thought" (*cogitatio caeca, pensée sourde* or *vuide*), "blind knowledge" (*cognitio caeca*), "suppositive notion" (*cognitio suppositiva, connaissance suppositive*) and even "suppositive notion" (*notio suppositiva*) and "blind concept" (*conceptus caecus*). The meaning of all these expressions is approximately the same. In general, they refer to an act of thought "without ideas", that in this way is opposed to a thought with ideas, that is, an "intuitive" thought.

The expression Leibniz preferred throughout the development of his philosophy was, by a long way, "blind thought". The use of this expression goes from de *Dissertatio de Arte Combinatoria* (1666) to the *Nouveaux Essais*, at least.[4] "Blind knowledge" (*cognitio caeca*) and "suppositive knowledge" (*cognitio suppositiva, suppositive connaissance*)[5] appear both in the late 80's, when he achieved a first systematic interconnection among his metaphysical, epistemological and logical conceptions. A few years after the publication of the *Meditationes*, Leibniz prefers the expression "suppositive knowledge" instead of "blind knowledge". Again, we find the terms "suppositive notion" (*notio suppositiva*) and "blind concept" (*conceptus caecus*) in two programmatic drafts on General Science and General Characteristic pertaining also to the referred period.[6] The context in which both expressions appear clearly shows that they have the same

---

[3] *Cognitio symbolica*: A VI 4, 585; *cogitatio symbolica*. A VI 4, 587-588.
[4] A VI 1, 170, 551; A VI 2, 481; A VI 4, 587; A VI 6, 185-186, 259, 275, 286.
[5] *Cognitio caeca*: A VI 4, 1815; *cognitio suppositiva/connaissance suppositive*: A VI 4, 1815; A VI 4, 1568; A VI 4, 1569.
[6] *Notio suppositiva*: A VI 4, 912; *conceptus caecus*: A VI 4, 973.

meaning as "blind thought". In conclusion, wordings such as "blind thought", "symbolic thought", "suppositive, blind or symbolic knowledge" or "suppositive notion" are practically equivalent to each other in meaning. In any case, "blind thought" is the expression that best fits the concept that Leibniz was trying to define and maybe for this reason Leibniz preferred to use it as a general denomination throughout his life. Summing up, if we try to determine what the term "symbolic knowledge" means for Leibniz, we have to direct our attention to the concept of "blind thought".

We can now anticipate our main conclusions about a possible characterization of the concept of blind thought. Indeed, the analysis of this concept will show that it can pose as many advantages as potentially dangerous factors for our knowledge. The positive aspects of "blind thought" are tied to the nature and function of the symbolic calculi (such as the arithmetical calculi and the algebraic methods for the solution of arithmetical and geometrical problems), while its negative aspects are connected with how we usually think or reason using ordinary language, that is, the language that we use everyday to communicate and express to the others our ideas and beliefs, either orally or in writing.

The first aspect of "blind thought" corresponds to what Sybille Krämer calls "operative symbolism" and was maybe what Leibniz was trying to capture with the expressions "symbolic knowledge" and "symbolic thought" in the *Meditationes*.[7] Nevertheless, as we shall see, we do not really obtain new cognitive content through operations with symbols; we order instead, transform and develop in a reliable way the knowledge that we have already obtained beforehand.

On the contrary, the second aspect of "blind thought", which represents its negative side, comes from the dangers that our ordinary linguistic comprehension implies for our cognitive claims, to the extent that we carry out intellectual processes and reasonings or communicate with the others by means of the words and sentences belonging to ordinary language. In fact, our usual linguistic comprehension of the spoken languages can hide falsehoods and mistakes that could pass unnoticed, in such a way that we could take for knowledge what is in fact ignorance and error.

Nevertheless, in both cases the use of symbols of some kind is an unavoidable condition for human thought. Indeed, according to Leibniz, the possibility of thinking depends in one way or another on symbols, whatever their nature may be. Thus, since symbols are perceptible (or at least imaginable) things, there has to be a close link between thought, perception and imagination. It follows from this a worrisome consequence: if our thinking is essentially bound to symbols, then are not our cognitive processes, our reasoning and, in general, all our thoughts somehow blind? And if it was so, how can Leibniz justify such an optimistic view about the performances of the (operative) symbolic systems for our knowledge? In

---

[7] Krämer **1997**, p. 112.

what follows, we try to approach and answer these questions and others that are intertwined with them.

Our general strategy in dealing with these questions will be to show, in the first place, how Leibniz introduces a bivalent characterization of blind thought or "symbolic knowledge", especially in the writings of his maturity. Then, we will try to prove that the ambiguous way in which Leibniz characterizes the performances of blind thought for our knowledge is the result of two different argumentative lines that can be traced back to writings that are prior to the *Meditationes* and even back to his first works. From this analysis we will reach the conclusion that the positive aspects of blind thought are closely connected with the concepts of symbolic notation and calculus. In this way, from the idea that symbolic knowledge, in its proper sense, is that which we obtain by means of notational symbolic systems in the style of arithmetic and algebra, we will explain both the diverse features that blind knowledge, understood as calculus, assumes and the foundation that Leibniz tries to give to it, as well as the problems that a unitary characterization of the concept has to face.

1. *Cognitio intuitiva* versus *cogitatio caeca* in Leibniz's mature philosophy

Let us sum up the main ideas about "blind thought" or "blind knowledge" such as they are presented in *Meditationes* and in the writings that came after it. In these writings, blind thought is clearly opposed to "intuitive thought" or "intuitive knowledge". Precisely, this opposition is approached in *Meditationes*, where it is presented as a confrontation between symbolic knowledge (or symbolic thought) and intuitive knowledge (or intuitive thought):

> Knowledge is either *obscure* or *clear*; clear knowledge is either *confused* or *distinct*; distinct knowledge is either *inadequate* or *adequate*, and also either *symbolic* or *intuitive*.[8]

In general terms, an obscure knowledge is a notion or concept that does not make possible the recognition of the thing about which we are thinking, whereas a clear knowledge does. In turn, clear but confused knowledge is a notion or concept that satisfies three basic conditions: first, it makes possible the recognition of the object of which it is a concept; moreover, its content has to be somehow given and, finally, this content cannot be elucidated, in the sense that we cannot define or analyze it by means of other concepts or notions, due to a limitation of our cognitive faculties. Thus, the appropriate way of obtaining these notions is by an ostensive indication, as it happens,

---

[8] *Meditationes*, A VI 4, 585-586 [Loemker 291].

for example, with basic empirical properties. In turn, distinct knowledge depends on a notion or concept that must possess as a fundamental mark that it is capable of explanation by means of an analysis of its conceptual components. Moreover, a notion is distinct but inadequate, if the non-analyzable notions that compound it are confused notions, so that our analysis must halt due to of a limitation of our cognitive power. On the contrary, distinct adequate knowledge is a notion or concept that is finitely analyzable in terms of other notions or concepts that are not analyzable, but this non-analyzability does not depend on a limitation of our cognitive power, but results from the very nature of such notions. Indeed, such concepts ought to be the simplest and in this way immediately knowable by themselves. Intuitive knowledge depends, in the final instance, on the existence of this kind of notion.

However, Leibniz acknowledges implicitly two types of intuitive knowledge. First of all, the concepts or notions that, being simple by their nature, are conceived by themselves are intuitive. Also intuitive are those complex notions that, being composed of intuitive concepts, can be known by conceiving simultaneously all and each of their intuitive conceptual components. Indeed, Leibniz introduces the concept of symbolic knowledge precisely in opposition to intuitive knowledge, especially of this just explained second type. In fact, when we cannot embrace in a unique apprehension the primitive simple concepts that constitute the adequate complex concept, we must resort to a way of thinking that has a "symbolic" feature:

> And indeed, when a concept is very complex, we certainly cannot think simultaneously of all the concepts which compose it. But when this is possible, or at least insofar as it is possible, I call the knowledge intuitive. There is no other knowledge of a distinct primitive concept than intuitive of a distinct primitive concept, while, for the most part, we have only symbolic thought of composites.[9]

In other words, symbolic thought appears when a concept is composite and so complex that we need to use signs to think of it. What distinguishes symbolic thought is that the intuitive apprehension of the primitive concepts in the act of thinking about a given item is not required, since all we need is the mediation of a sign or sensible mark, the symbol - a word or some other

---

[9] *Meditationes*, A VI 4, 588 [Loemker 292]; cfr. A VI 4, 544, A VI 4, 1568. Observe that Leibniz's denomination vacillates between "symbolic knowledge" (cfr. n. 2) and "symbolic thought". It can be a significant distinction. For the sake of simplicity, we take both expressions as equivalent.

kind of image - that is accompanied by a vague and confused comprehension of its meaning. Thus, our symbolic thought or knowledge is that to which we in general resort to when we make inferences, either in everyday life or in the practice of sciences, as the examples of the arithmetic operations or the algebraic reasoning show.[10]

Thus, "symbolic" or "blind" thought consists in the utilization of a certain sign, whose function is to substitute or "surrogate" the consideration of the ideas in themselves that correspond to the objects they stand for.[11] Observe, however, that even if Leibniz seems to present at the first sight symbolic thought or knowledge only as a surrogate of intuitive knowledge, its scope goes far beyond the latter, since its application is not restricted to the domain of mathematics, which is the kind of human knowledge that best fits the ideal of intuitive knowledge. In other words, the distinction between symbolic knowledge and the consideration of the "concepts in themselves" takes place not only within the adequate knowledge, but also affects the entire field of the distinct knowledge and even of the confused knowledge, since we appeal to signs in order to refer to both adequate notions and inadequate or confused notions, that is, everything that is included in the range of what is capable of being expressed, meant or referred to by means of signs. In conclusion, a table exhibiting the complete extension of the symbolic or "blind" thought must have the following double-entry structure:

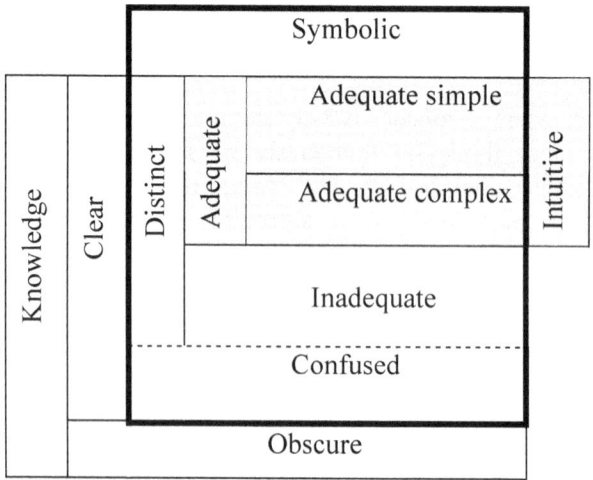

The grey zone indicates the domain of intuitive knowledge. The dotted line shows the continuity between confused and inadequate knowledge. The bold square points out the scope of symbolic knowledge.

---

[10] *Meditationes*, A VI 4, 587-588 [Loemker 292].
[11] Indeed, in order to be more precise, we must distinguish between a notion and an idea. For this topic, s. Poser **1979**.

Independently of the way in which symbolic knowledge relates to the other kinds of knowledge, we can extract from our previous considerations some important conclusions concerning our central question. Indeed, a preliminary characterization of what Leibniz understands by symbolic or blind knowledge can be summed up in the following factors: the surrogation factor, the semantic-intentional factor and the semiotic factor.

In a first approach, it can be said that symbolic or "blind" knowledge substitutes the consideration of the "ideas in themselves", in the sense that the sign stands for the idea as such. In this way, it carries out a surrogative function, since it uses words or some other kind of sign in the place of notions. In other words, we think signs, not notions, concepts or ideas and, by this reason, we can speak of a "symbolic thought". Concerning the semantic-intentional factor, symbolic or blind thought involves a vague or confused comprehension of the meaning of the symbols, for example, of the words, but not an exact and actual knowledge of the ideas that the words mean (which would constitute knowledge by ideas).[12] Certainly we believe that we can actualize at will in our minds the ideas referred to and suppose that we possess such knowledge of the ideas. For this reason we confidently use symbols, either words or other kinds of expressions. This is the reason why Leibniz calls such kind of thought 'blind' (and perhaps the reason why he avoids the denomination "blind knowledge"). The semiotic factor is represented by the dependence of the human thought on signs. Symbolic or blind thought is almost a necessary condition for our thinking, especially when complex intellectual processes are involved, which include complicated conceptual connections. Precisely, one of the outcomes of this substitutive function of symbolic or blind thought is the abbreviation of intellectual operations.

However, there is a risk that appears to undermine our confidence in symbolic thought. Because, namely, our vague and confused comprehension of the meaning of a word can lead us to believe that we know something or that we have the idea of something, when what really happens is that there is nothing that can be the object of our knowledge, since the meaning of the symbol that we think involves a contradictory concept. Thus, we can understand the meaning of a word or composition of words, but without knowing anything by it, since there is no idea of that which entails a contradiction. If knowledge is nothing more than thinking with ideas, blind thought expose us to the risk of making mistakes and incurring in falsities. This is the case of our everyday use of ordinary language, when we do not sufficiently examine the meanings of the words and uncritically accept the common understanding that we have of them.[13]

Let us denominate 'uncertainty factor' the fact that symbolic or blind thought can lead us to mistakes, due precisely to the fact that we believe we

---

[12] See n. 10.
[13] *Meditationes*, A VI 4, 588.

have an idea that in fact we do not. It is important to remember at this point that Leibniz establishes a distinction between 'concept' or 'notion' on the one hand and 'idea', on the other.[14] A concept is a content that is present to our thought, whereas an idea is a power of thinking. Thus, we can have a blind concept, even an impossible concept, but not an impossible idea.[15] In any case, we find in this point a negative aspect of symbolic or blind thought, about which we have spoken at the beginning: it can be erroneous because of its vacuity.

Perhaps this was the reason why Lebiniz abandoned the denomination 'symbolic thought' or 'symbolic knowledge' after the publication of the *Meditationes* and replaced it by 'blind thought', an usual denomination for him, or by a new designation, 'suppositive knowledge' (at least in one case, 'suppositive concept'). Precisely, this is the denomination that appears in the *Discourse de métaphysique*, as replacement of the expression 'symbolic thought', that we find in the *Meditationes*. As in the *Meditationes*, it means the surrogative thought of an idea by means of a sign (either a word or another kind of symbol), without the actual consideration or contemplation of the idea in itself. Thus, we suppose we have the knowledge of the idea, but in fact we do not know whether it is correct or not. Because of this, our knowledge is only putative knowledge and for this reason he denominates it 'suppositive'.[16] This qualification precisely expresses the uncertainty factor that we have just mentioned.

Finally, if we consider the way in which Leibniz deals with the same problem in the *Nouveaux Essais*, we find that the attributes of symbolic thought in the *Meditationes* or the ones of the 'suppositive knowledge' in the *Discourse of métaphysique* are taken up again under the concept of 'blind thought', that is, after all, the denomination that Leibniz applied in his youth for thought without ideas. Thus, blind thoughts (*pensées sourdes ou vuides, cogitationes caecas*) are empty of any perception or sensibility and consist in the use of characters, as is the case when calculating arithmetically or algebraically, or when using words, reasoning with the help of our ordinary language. In both cases, the object is absent from our minds and it is replaced by a sign.[17] Moreover, in blind thought there is a kind of vague or confused comprehension of what is signified by the words, even if our thought may be empty or blind.[18] However, the vacuity of blind thought is a source of mistakes and for this reason it can be the cause of uncertainty.[19] Even if it involves dangers for the soundness of our knowledge, it is an

---

[14] Poser **1979**, p. 312.

[15] A VI 4, 972.

[16] I have found only one text in which Leibniz uses the expression 'blind knowledge', with a meaning equivalent to 'suppositive knowledge'. It appears in a note to Malebranche (A VI 4, 1815).

[17] NE, A VI 6, 185-186; A VI 6, 259.

[18] NE, A VI 6, 286.

[19] NE, A VI 6, 259.

almost indispensable instrument for our thinking, since without it we cannot advance in our reasoning about practically any question.[20]

The fact that blind thought can hide contradictions seems to be not very favourable to the purpose that guides us, namely, the investigation of the relevance of the Leibnizian concept of blind thought with the aim of grounding the efficiency that symbolic languages possess in order to assure the expansion and foundation of our knowledge. In fact, given the negative features of blind thought, we could extract sceptical conclusions from the clear statements of Leibniz about the dependence of the human thought on signs, whether words, characters or images.[21]

If blind thought is a necessary condition for human thought and knowledge, it would seem that Leibniz ought to conclude from this thesis sceptical consequences about the possibility of knowledge, because of the uncertainty factor that affects the resort to symbolic thought. But in fact, and to a great extent, Leibniz trusts the possibilities that the "operative symbolism" opens up for the enlargement and foundation of our knowledge. Moreover, the whole of his project on the Universal or General Characteristics turns on the concept of blind thought. Do we face in this point a contradiction?[22] Will it not be possible to speak of 'blind knowledge' after all?

In what follows, I will try to show the possibility of the concept of blind knowledge, despite of the difficulties that we have pointed out. With this aim, we have to re-examine the concept of blind thought in order to restrict the scope of the concept of symbolic knowledge. As we shall see, not all blind thought is a source of uncertainty. In fact, the remarkable advancement of mathematical sciences is based, according to Leibniz, on blind thought such as it is represented by arithmetical or algebraic symbolism. Now, the reliability of the mathematical notations depends on the way in which they are construed as symbolic systems. Thus, symbolic knowledge is a kind of knowledge that results from the application of symbolic systems that are devised according to the general model of algebraic notation.

Before developing our analysis, I would like to return briefly to the question about the denominations 'symbolic thought' and 'symbolic knowledge' in the *Meditationes*. Why did Leibniz replace his usual and well established denomination 'blind thought' by this new 'symbolic thought'? We propose the following answer: Leibniz proceeded in this way following a suggestion that he found in the writings of Joachim Jungius. In fact, denominations such as *notio symbolica, conceptus symbolicus, conceptus symbolaris* (among other names, Jungius also uses *notio titularis* and *notio kenonymica*) appear in the *Logica de Notionibus*, from which Leibniz

---

[20] NE, A VI 6, 275.
[21] NE, A VI 6, 77, GP 3, 466; Bodemann 97.
[22] A distinction between Universal Characteristic and General Characteristic is introduced later on in this work.

extracted copious notes by the time of the *Meditationes*.[23] And what is more important is the fact that the meaning that Jungius gives to these expressions coincides with the Leibnizian notion of 'blind thought'. Indeed, for Jungius, a symbolic notion consists in the consideration of a thing by means of the use of a name, without thinking the aggregate of concepts that constitute the definition of the referred thing. We act in this way –says Jungius-, in order to think quickly and shortly, knowing that we can recall the constituting concepts at will. This kind of notion plays an important and necessary function in mathematical reasoning and thinking in general. Anyway, although the symbolic concept is necessary, it can be the cause of mistakes, since it can induce us to believe falsely that we possess a concept that we do not actually have.[24] In conclusion, there are so many coincidences between the views of Jungius and Leibniz that Leibniz himself added the following observation to the text of Jungius: "These statements replicate my own." Thus, Leibniz's denomination 'symbolic thought' could be inspired by the remarkable overlapping between the points of view that Jungius and Leibniz maintained on the uses, utility and dangers of the signs for the intellectual processes.

2. Two sorts of 'blind thought'

In what follows, I would like to sustain the following hypothesis: if we consider what Leibniz has said about blind thought since his first philosophical essays, we can find two main streams of development concerning this concept. The first line of development is fundamentally associated to the use of characters or symbols in the operations of the arithmetical or algebraic calculus. On the contrary, the second line is tied to our linguistic comprehension that is proper of our use of ordinary language in our communication with others or in our lonely reasoning with ourselves.[25] The main advantage of the first form of blind thought, which we call 'symbolic blind thought' (from now on 'Symbolic Thought'), consists in providing a guide to our thinking, for ordering our knowledge and developing the formal relationships that are involved in its contents. Moreover, in order to achieve these aims, we do not need to understand the material meanings of the expressions (although the recognition of categories of symbols, that is, "intrasymbolic meanings", according to Krämer's

---

[23] *Logica de Notionibus. Jungiarum schedarum excerpta annotata*, A VI 4, 1211-1299. The *excerpta* and observations are dated in 1685 approximately. If our hypothesis is right, perhaps they could be earlier.
[24] A VI 4, 1291-1292.
[25] See the distinction that M. Serfati **2005**, following Cajori **1928/29**, introduces between a rhetorical and a symbolic tradition, which begins with Viète and Descartes, in the practice of mathematics.

terminology, is not excluded),[26] but it is only required that we follow the rules of the symbolic operations. For this reason, symbolic systems must be "well constructed". A very important feature of Symbolic Thought is that we make use of written characters that can be seen or at least visually imagined.

As it has been said before, from the concept of 'Symbolic Thought' derives the Leibnizian project about a Universal or General Characteristic, that is, a generalization of the operative symbolism that characterizes arithmetic and algebra. On the contrary, the second form of blind thought, which is blind thought in ordinary language (for this reason we will call it 'Verbal Thought' from now on), affects fundamentally the use of languages that are depending on the articulation of words and are essentially phonic. In opposition to the arithmetical and algebraic symbolisms, which are artificial in a general sense, such languages have arisen spontaneously in the history of mankind from the need for communication imposed by social life, after which they were developed as an instrument for the reasoning. Thus, we resort to them when we are in need of communication with each other or when we are reasoning alone.

For this reason, in the ordinary languages, vocal signs or acoustic images predominate over written characters, although Verbal Thought can share some of the features of Symbolic Thought when a system of writing has been developed for it. In opposition to Symbolic Thought, Verbal Thought requires a certain comprehension of the "extrasymbolic" meanings, although it would be confused, vague or erratic. In other words, in Verbal Thought we need what we have denominated in the analysis of the *Meditationes* the semantic-intentional factor of the symbolic thought. Nevertheless, it is in this last factor where we find the main source of the weakness of Verbal Thought, for it generally entails a confused meaning comprehension, which, as we have just seen, can infect our thinking with hidden falsities, contradictions or chimerical notions. Both the Leibnizian analysis of Verbal Thought and the criticism that he addresses against this kind of blind thought culminate in his theory of definition, the examination of which exceeds the scope of this work and for this reason we will not deal with it here.[27] Finally, both forms of conceiving blind thought converge in the *Meditationes*, in the *Discours de métaphysique* and in the *Nouveaux Essais*, bringing about in this way the ambiguous status that we have detected in the Leibnizian description of the concept.

Certainly, we will not attempt at fully reconstructing the development of both streams of thought about the topic, but we will limit ourselves to pointing out certain landmarks of this development through the texts in which Leibniz deals explicitly with blind thought according to one or other of its two versions (Symbolic Thought or Verbal Thought).

---

[26] Krämer **1991**, p 325.
[27] For the development of Leibniz's theory of definition, see Dascal **1978** and Dascal **1980**, especially in connection with the "formal approach" to the concept of symbolic knowledge.

Thus, in the *Dissertatio de Arte Combinatoria* (1666) (from now on *Dissertatio*) occurs one of the first, if not the first, mention of the *cogitatio caeca* understood as Symbolic Thought in the works of Leibniz.[28] The occurrence takes place in the context of the introduction of the central concepts for the constitution of the new method, namely, the Combinatorial, in which number plays a central role, since the core of the method depends precisely on the calculus of the arithmetical Combinatorial. In the introductory paragraphs, where concepts such as variation and complexion are defined,[29] Leibniz characterizes number as a form of blind thought. Both the variations and the complexions pertain to the theory of wholes and parts. Therefore, since the parts that constitute the wholes can be numerated, it is possible to apply numbers in order to carry out a surrogative handling of the relations between wholes and parts. This gives rise to the idea that anticipates a fundamental aspect of the Leibnizian conceptions on symbolic representation: the number is a kind of "universal picture" by means of which everything, whatever may be its nature, can be represented and dealt with.[30] An outstanding example of the symbolic performance of number is given by the numerical notations, since we can understand a numerical expression without the necessity of conceiving intuitively the unities that compose the number signified by this expression:

> For example, we often grasp a number, however large, all at once in a kind of *blind thought*, namely, when we read ciphers on paper which not even the age of Methusela would suffice to count explicitly.[31]

Further, since number is the quantity of the parts, we can think the whole as the collective and abstract unity of its parts with the help of number, that is, of blind thought.[32] Thus, number (and the numerical expression that represents it, the act of unification or recollection) constitutes the abstract form of a whole. What is more, since anything that can be numerated, it can be considered in its turn as a whole (because the form of a whole is simply the possibility of being conceived conjointly by the mind), Leibniz concludes that number becomes the maximally universal form for everything.[33] Therefore, blind thought, as represented by the numerical notation, allows us to operate surrogatively with the abstract form of a whole. In this way, it makes possible the application of arithmetic to the entire domain of the world, whether material or spiritual. In this sense,

---

[28] A VI 1, 170-171.
[29] A VI 1, 171.
[30] *Ibidem.*
[31] A VI 1, 170 [Loemker 76, my italics].
[32] *Ibidem.*
[33] A VI 1, 171.

Leibniz connects his own combinatorial project with the Cartesian tradition of Universal Mathematics or *analytica speciosa*.[34]

In conclusion, the concept of blind thought is introduced in the *Dissertatio* through the analysis of the fundamental role played by numerical expressions for the universal method, thus demonstrating in a preliminary and implicit way, the surrogative function and the operative nature of arithmetical notation, both of which express fundamental features of Symbolic Thought.

Another step towards the elucidation of the significance of Symbolic Thought for Leibniz is contained in the considerations of a brief essay, dated between 1671 and 1672, whose title is *Demonstratio Propositionum Primarum*. Whereas the mention of Symbolic Thought in the *Dissertatio* is rather incidental, the *Demonstratio* develops in a quite detailed fashion the function that symbols fulfil in mathematical demonstrations. Thus, the outcome of the analysis is the affirmation that Symbolic Thought provides a kind of structural or formal frame that orders our knowledge, but does not produce new cognitive contents. In this way, the analysis suggests an idea which will be consolidated during the development of Leibniz's thought. Certainly, the view that Symbolic Thought is based on order expresses incipiently the structural character of symbolic knowledge, as we shall see later.

The main problem by virtue of which the treatment of Symbolic Thought is dealt with in the *Demonstratio* centers on our capability –enigmatic to some degree- for discovering or inventing theorems by means of the use of signs. As already explained by Leibniz in the *Dissertatio*, definitions are the clue for the demonstrative discovery of new propositions, because demonstrations are no more than chains of definitions, whereas definitions are chains of words (or signs).[35] Therefore, we can obtain demonstrations by the combination of definitions and the reciprocal substitution between *definientia* and *definienda*. Now, if the demonstration would consist solely in such a procedure, the discovery or invention of new theorems would be of no use, since we would not know anything of new, because everything would be already contained beforehand in the definitions.[36] In fact, we obtain new combinations of words and even new words, but not new contents. Therefore, we do not learn anything new that goes beyond what we had at the beginning.

Leibniz's answer to this difficulty entails a reflection about the use of signs, especially of the arithmetical symbols and, thus, of Symbolic Thought. When we learn to count or to calculate with the help of numerals, we do not know in fact new contents, but conceive of a collection of unities in

---

[34] *Ibidem*.
[35] A VI 2, 479.
[36] A VI 2, 480.

abbreviated form and operate with it.[37] It is important to consider the implications of the function of abbreviation that numerals fulfil. On the one hand, such function expresses the dependence of the human mind on the use of signs due to the limitations of our memory.[38] On the other hand, it shows that signs play a surrogative function, since the operation with numerical expressions is so reliable that we do not need to think on the concrete unities that form the collection in order to bring about the computation. In other words, we can draw conclusions about the properties and relations of the collections of unities by reasoning surrogatively on the numerals.[39] The same happens in the demonstrations: when we find a theorem through a demonstration, we do no more than arrange our knowledge in an orderly and abbreviated way to be able to conceive it at once with a quick movement of our thinking. Indeed, if we had to always redefine each word or sign at each step of our demonstration, thinking would be impossible. Thus, Symbolic Thought provide us a means to briefly and surrogatively consider a complicated question, composed by many elements, and in this sense, it is a fundamental condition of human thought, given its natural limitations:

> Thus, nobody could carry out in his mind reasonings that are extremely lengthy, had not certain signs been invented, that is, names by means of which the overwhelming amount of things should be embraced in such abbreviated way that this multitude can be gone through. Such thing would be impossible if, by suppressing names or other signs like these, definitions were to be used in the place of that defined. And I use to call such thoughts blind. Nothing is more necessary or frequent for man than them.[40]

There is another condition that Leibniz demands for Symbolic Thought, namely, order condition. Symbolic Thought can become a reliable guide for thinking only under the condition that the symbolic expressions are built up according to a certain order. Again, the example of the numerals gives us a clue of the requisites that Symbolic Thought has to match in order to efficiently fulfil its surrogative and psychotecnic function.[41] Numerals are constituted according to certain rules of construction and transformation that warrant (or ought to warrant) the cogency of the arithmetical operations that are executed with their intervention. By means of the application of such

---

[37] A VI 2, 481.
[38] See Dascal **1978**, especially chap. VI.
[39] A VI 2, 481.
[40] *Ibidem.*
[41] The psychotecnic function consists in discharching the work of the memory. The term is taken from Dascal **1978**, 173-174 *et passim.*

rules a symbolic order is constructed that is 'structure preserving' and, at the same time, simplifies our thinking processes.[42]

Since the effectiveness of Symbolic Thought depends on order and, in this sense, contains implicitly a structural knowledge, Leibniz concludes that the symbolic constructions that are obtained through symbolic transformations have only a formal significance. They do not constitute an increment of cognitive content, but only exhibit in a condensed and distinct fashion the complexity of the relations that are involved and hidden by itself in a plurality of objects. Furthermore, this structural feature of Symbolic Thought sustains its psychotechnic function, in the sense that an abbreviated operation of thought is made possible by the syntactical order and transformation of the symbols.[43]

Summing up, symbolic thought that follows the paradigm of symbolic calculus of arithmetic and algebra does not entail an increase of content in our knowledge, but only orders it. Nevertheless, it enables us to transform, to develop and to compare the formal relations that otherwise would remain hidden and virtual in the cognitive contents that we have held beforehand. Symbolic systems that are correctly constructed are machines for processing knowledge. From this point of view, they contain only a syntactical or structural knowledge, although it may remain implicit:

> For this reason we see that those who possess the art of employing the right words in a constant way tend to reason, that is, to order their thoughts exactly. The reasoning and the demonstration do not increase the thoughts, but they order them. The usefulness of a theorem is no more than to say a great amount of things in an abbreviated way. And the more abbreviated the more suitable for its application. Indeed, when a multitude of things is expressed in a shortened way at once, they can be compared and gone through easily, and at the same time they can be coordinated towards a single purpose, that is, the solving of problems.[44]

Note that even if the paradigm of the calculus represents a dominant factor in the formulation of the concept of Symbolic Thought, it is not exclusive. In fact, Leibniz considers the possibility that Symbolic Thought takes place in the domain of words and not only in the symbolic languages of arithmetic and algebra. Perhaps such observation could represent an objection to our efforts to make a distinction between two sorts of blind

---

[42] *Ibidem*.
[43] A VI 3, 426-427. See *Accessio ad arithmeticam infinitorum*, A III 1, 13-14.
[44] A VI 2, 481-482.

thought, one of them associated to the idea of calculus and the other tied more to ordinary language. However, it is worth noting that the use of words in the demonstrations is conditioned by a very strong restriction, namely, that of the meanings of the words must be specified by means of explicit definitions. Certainly, already since the time of the *Dissertatio*, definitions are for Leibniz one of the fundamental elements for the demonstrations. In other words, expressions and propositions of ordinary language can become cases of Symbolic Thought on condition that they are regimented, as in the case of the usual geometrical demonstrations, where definitions and axioms are stated in the words of ordinary language, but in a rigorous way. From this point of view, this 'special' use of ordinary language departs from the usual and common use of words, and for this reason we can conceive it as being very close to the algorithmic ideal of Symbolic Thought, with which it has tended to merge since the time of the *Dissertatio*.

As we have seen, Symbolic Thought does not require that there necessarily be comprehension of the meaning. On the other hand, the orderly disposition of the signs is decisive for Symbolic Thought in order to achieve its goal. Such a disposition is obtained by the application of rules for the construction and transformation of the symbolic expressions. It does not matter so much whether or not we understand the extrasymbolic meanings of the signs, because we do not need to take account of their meanings to operate with symbolic expressions. All that is required from us is that we correctly apply the right rules.

However, there are others contexts in which resorting to linguistic signs implies the necessity of understanding extralinguistic meanings, although we still have to think 'blindly'. This is the case fundamentally when we appeal to ordinary language in everyday life in our social interchanges or in our meditation. In such situations we face another form of blind thought that is characterised by the fact that we have a vague and confused comprehension of the meanings of the words and sentences, with no possibility of better specifying that meaning. Thus, our mind moves so to say in a milieu of diffused linguistic comprehension in which meaning cannot be established univocally and firmly.

It is notable that Leibniz approaches this rather negative side of blind thought in ordinary language (Verbal Thought) when he deals with the problems that the right interpretation of the biblical texts presents and thus the questions about the truth of faith, which, by their very nature, are subjected to a variety of interpretations that can be mutually incompatible, as is the case of the Eucharist. Precisely a brief essay titled *Commentatiuncula de judice controversiarum, seu trutina rationis et norma textus*, dated between 1669 and 1671, concerns this matter.[45]

At first sight, the text deals with a practical question that can be formulated in this way: what does a layman understand or should

---

[45] A VI 1, 548-559.

understand, when claiming to believe in the mystery of the Eucharist, especially when there is a multiplicity of interpretations about what the New Testament tells us about it? Indeed, belief in the sacrament based on the comprehension of its enunciation has to be distinguished from its merely verbal repetition without any comprehension.[46] Thus, believing in something entails assuming the truth of what we believe and, for this reason, a minimal condition for this is to grasp the meaning of the sentence that enunciates the fact that we accept.[47] But since there are controversies about the precise meaning of statements such a "this is my body", in what sense has the layman to take Jesus' affirmation without falling into specific heresy? We can find the answer in the nature of Verbal Thought: The layman's obligation is to believe *in bona fide* what the Bible says, taking the words in the vague and diffused meaning according to which we use them in our everyday linguistic interchanges. Furthermore, concerning the exact meaning of the sentences, we have to leave the question undecided, so that we may glide, so to say, among different interpretations, without pronouncing ourselves categorically in favour of one or the other.[48] What seems to be a weakness of Verbal Thought becomes here an advantage: the confused thinking by means of a verbal sign makes it possible for us to believe in a truth without engaging us in an explicit doctrine or theory of a fact that by itself is not understandable. Concerning the practice of faith, Verbal Thought allows us to be truthful believers without the risks of the entanglements in theological controversies.

Notwithstanding, Verbal Thought is applied not only in practical questions, as happens in the practice of religious life, but also in our everyday reflections on theoretical questions. In fact, even the most common of mortals appeal to Verbal Thought when they meditate on truth, existence and other questions like these.[49] This kind of thought can also take its own place in our daily life, even when we apply theoretical concepts (like 'cause' or 'truth') in our unreflecting dealing with practical issues. However, for philosophical theoretical knowledge, Verbal Thought involves a severe danger, namely, the threat of talking equivocally and metaphorically about things about which we have actually no genuine understanding. Indeed, what for the practice of faith was an advantage now becomes a setback for theoretical thinking. As we have seen, meanings in Verbal Thought are loaded with a high degree of confusion and uncertainty, from which philosophical terms also suffer, like for example 'cause', especially in the use that philosophers like Aristotle or the Scholastics make of them, because they do not accurately and distinctly define the meanings of these philosophical terms and, when they do, they resort only to metaphors, as can

---

[46] A VI 1, 551.
[47] A VI 1, 550.
[48] A VI 1, 550-551.
[49] A VI 1, 551.

be seen from the work of Suárez.[50] Therefore, the conclusion is unavoidable that the use of Verbal Thought in philosophy can mislead us by providing our thinking with false confidence. As we have seen, Leibniz considers that these disadvantages can be eliminated by an adequate regimentation of meanings by means of definitions, but it is only half a solution, to the extent that there are not clear criteria of what a right definition is. Nevertheless, by the time of the *Commentatiuncula* Leibniz had not yet developed a satisfactory theory of definition, the need for which was to become more and more pressing in the 1680's and was to achieve in the *Meditations* its definitive form through the distinction between nominal and real definitions. Whatever the case, the introduction of explicit definitions represents a step towards another way of thinking, that of Symbolic Thought.

3. The features of Symbolic Thought

The analysis that we have performed so far has revealed two Leibnizian views on blind thought, namely, according to our denomination, Symbolic Thought and Verbal Thought view, respectively. Both views eventually merge later in the ambivalent description of the *Meditationes*. Nonetheless, it must be acknowledged that we have presented only a partial picture of the issue, since for a complete treatment of it we should analyse Leibniz's theory of definition, whose complexity exceeds the scope of our exposition. However, in spite of the importance of the question about definitions,[51] we would like to concentrate on the concept of Symbolic Thought, in order to spell out its distinctive features. Since according to our view the Leibnizian concept of symbolic knowledge is grounded on the performances of Symbolic Thought, we will from now on use symbolic knowledge to refer to the kind of knowledge that is obtained by means of Symbolic Thought, independently of the terminological decisions that Leibniz has chosen.

Let us summarize some of the basic features of Symbolic Thought that we discovered during our textual analysis about the differences between Symbolic Thought and Verbal Thought.

One of the advantages of Symbolic Thought is represented by the abbreviating function it fulfils for cognitive operations. By means of this feature, that we call 'psychotechnic function',[52] Symbolic Thought performs the task of improving the work of our memory by reducing the amount of data that it has to deal with. As a part of it, symbolic expressions have the virtue of 'leading' or 'guiding' the inferential processes. For this reason, Leibniz calls the properly devised symbolic expressions *"filum cogitandi"*

---

[50] *Ibidem.*
[51] See note 64.
[52] See note 40.

that is, a thread for thinking.[53] This performance is one of the main features of the algorithmic symbolic systems and makes up a core motive of the program of the Characteristic. The surrogative function is also another aspect that stands out clearly in our analysis: Symbolic Thought substitutes the direct dealing with "the things themselves". Finally, a third mark arises from our examination: although Symbolic Thought does not produce new cognitive content, it introduces order in the knowledge that we already possess, so that we can deal more easily with it and develop the complicated relations that are involved in it. This feature, that we have called 'structural', compensates deficiencies involved in Verbal Thought. In fact, the order that is established both among the symbols of the arithmetical calculus and among the *definientia* and the *definienda* when a regimented language is utilised guarantees the correctness of our conclusions, although we cannot consider effectively and directly the objects signified by them. This quality of Symbolic Thought has as a consequence that cognitive operations tend to gain independence from the need of grasping meanings when we are engaged in thinking, which was an important restriction of Verbal Thought. Furthermore, the setting up of an order opens a way for overcoming the uncertainty factor that is introduced in Verbal Thought by the vagueness and confusion of the verbal meanings. In other words, order is what makes Symbolic Thought become a reliable cognitive operation. Nevertheless, we haven't yet analysed the nature of such an order, although the arithmetical paradigm points towards the kind of 'operational' order furnished by the examples of the arithmetical and algebraic symbolism.[54]

In the texts we have analysed until now some of these ideas are clearly formulated, whereas others are rather sketchy and appear incidentally. In what follows, we try to outline more accurately the shape that these first insights by Leibniz on Symbolic Thought assume in his later intellectual development. In first place, we approach the idea that Symbolic Thought is a kind of making perceptible, a "sensualization", of our thoughts so that the execution of cognitive operations are reduced to a handling with and regarding physical objects, that are no more than symbolic expressions.

The idea that written symbols or notations furnish a "perceptible thread" for our thinking is already involved in Leibniz's description of number as a "universal picture" in the *Dissertatio*. The emphasis with which Leibniz stresses since his early writings the importance of pictures and diagrams in the exposition of sciences can be similarly interpreted.[55] Indeed, as the project of the Characteristic gradually acquires its shape, especially during the 1670s and particularly since the *Accessio ad arithmeticam infinitorum*

---

[53] See note 65 and ss.
[54] The 'operational' order is anticipated already in the *Dissertatio*, where Leibniz, following the suggestion of Hobbes, conceives of the thinking according to the model or the arithmetical operations. A VI 1, 194.
[55] *Totos libros explicare una figura* (1670-1671), A VI 1, 477.

from 1672,[56] the visualization function of symbolic languages and therefore of Symbolic Thought receives an explicit formulation.

In fact, in the *Accessio* we again find the same features of Symbolic Thought that we have dealt with in early texts. In first place, by means of Symbolic Thought we set up an order among already known ideas. Furthermore, these symbolic orders make it possible to devise abbreviated methods for thinking.[57] For this reason, both arithmetic and algebra best exemplify the psychotechnic and structuring function of Symbolic Thought. In fact, algebra makes it possible to reduce the treatment of a problem to the resolution of an equation by means of the mere transposition of symbols. Thus, one can arrive at the idea of Symbolic Thought as "operative thinking". From this point of view, algebra as a paradigmatic case of "operative thinking" fulfils a psychotechnic function and, at the same time, has a structural nature.

Indeed, algebra enables operation with highly complex relations and connections, since through its methods of representation "...a question is exhibited naked to the mind".[58] Thus, a new quality of algebra as well as of Symbolic Thought appears: the algebraic characters show, that is, allow us to visualize relations that otherwise would remain hidden to us who operate with them. As Leibniz says, through symbols "...one can observe a lot of things that otherwise one cannot see..." Thus, symbolic notation of algebra displays the formal structure of a question that thus becomes apparent to us. Since algebra is basically a writing or notation, clearly the structural feature of Symbolic Thought is tightly tied up to the composition of the formula as a physical object. By this means, the displaying function or *ad oculos* feature of symbolic expressions is added to their operational function. The possibility of visualizing inferential procedures by means of symbols is, for Leibniz, the decisive trait in which is grounded the success of mathematics, especially algebra, and that he demands for every symbolic system that tries to fulfil the ideal of the concept of Symbolic Thought.[59]

Summing up, to the psychotechnic, surrogative and structural factors have to be added two new aspects of Symbolic Thought: its visual nature and its displaying function, which must be understood in the sense that the symbolic structure makes visible, "shows" an interconnection of structural relations. The operative feature of Symbolic Thought makes it possible to operate on and with the formula, without the need of considering the ideas that, as contents, are connected by these relations. In this view, Leibniz applies the typical example of the positional numerical notation as surrogate of the unities that compose the symbolised number.[60] Nevertheless, although

---

[56] A III 1, 1-20.
[57] A III 1, 13.
[58] *Ibidem*.
[59] *Elementa rationis*, A VI 4, 714.
[60] A III 1, 17.

thus these features seem to reinforce the 'blind' nature of Symbolic Thought, we will see that Symbolic Thought can become not so 'blind'.

Finally, arithmetic, algebra and the definitional method introduced already in the *Dissertatio*[61] furnish the basis for conceiving Symbolic Thought according to the model of a machine. In this way, operation with symbols leads to the view on thinking as a mechanical or automatic procedure consisting in the regulated construction and transformation of symbolic structures, without the need of intentional reference to objects or meanings. Thus Leibniz proposes a computational model for Symbolic Thought and by its means the program for the Characteristic, which results from the generalization of the advantages of the Symbolic Thought such that they are exemplified in arithmetic and algebra to every kind of knowledge. One of the main benefits of the Characteristic is, precisely, the possibility of achieving mechanical demonstrations and the elimination of mistakes in reasoning:[62]

> Therefore, since our mind could be discharged to such a high degree by means of adequately invented symbols, in the manner of a spiritual machine, and since the things that are in our hands are however not ordered nor simple, except in the pure mathematical sciences..., one has to conclude that concerning every human reasoning nobody could deserve more merit than the man who designs either a language or a philosophical writing... that should be at the service solely of rigorous investigation.[63]

In few words, the views of the *Accessio* are continued with the concepts on Symbolic Thought that were put forward in early writings and develop explicitly aspects that could be implicitly suggested in them. Whatever it may be, the resulting features of Symbolic Thought can be formulated according to the following points:

1. Symbolic Thought requires symbolic structures considered as systems of physical objects subjected to operations of construction and transformation according to rules. Thus, Symbolic Thought is tied to the view that conceives of thinking as a kind of computing or calculating and, by this means, to the project of constructing symbolic systems that

---

[61] It is worth emphasizing that in the *Accessio* Leibniz conceives definition as a kind of equation: A III, 1, 18: "In this Universal Characteristic definitions are the same as equations in algebra".
[62] A III 1, 14-15.
[63] A III 1, 17-18.

reduce inferences to regulated symbolic transformations. Thus we would obtain the *filum mechanicum meditandi*.

2. Symbolic expressions of Symbolic Thought are basically notations or writings that have as a main feature the visual displaying of structural relations of the objects in question. This idea shall be developed later in the metaphor of the 'picture of the thought' or 'of the truth'. Moreover, this feature of Symbolic Thought constitutes an important factor that contributes to shape its structural or formal nature.

3. From the psychotechnic point of view, Symbolic Thought is a means for releasing our memory and for making our cognitive operations easier. By means of it, the power of human understanding is increased and improved. This advantage of Symbolic Thought is expressed in the Leibniz' view of a generalized calculus as an instrument for expanding the power of reason.

4. Symbolic Thought also has a surrogative function, as long as operations with and on the symbolic expression substitutes the direct contemplation of the ideas that are involved in the treatment of a problem or question.

5. Symbolic Thought eliminates or at least reduces the possibility of mistakes, since our thinking is guided by the rules of construction and operation of the calculus. When definitions are used, they determine the meanings, that is, the equivalences between characters or names, whereas the rules of symbolic transformation do the rest of the work.[64]

---

[64] This definition presents especial problems for the Symbolic Thought that Leibniz had not yet approached by the time of the *Accessio*. Initially, definitions play a fundamental role in the Leibnizian view on demonstration. Indeed, definitions constitute a point of depart from which true propositions can be obtained by mutually substituting *defniniens* and *definiendum* by each other. From the point of view of the Symbolic Thought (and the project of the Universal Characteristic too), definition fulfils both a syntactical and semantic function. Concerning the syntactical function, the definition sets up an equivalence between strings of symbols so that they can be replaced reciprocally by each other, independently of their semantic content. From the semantic point of view, the definition introduces an analysis of the idea meant by the *definiens* in terms of the ideas meant by characters or names of the *definiendum*. Once definitions are adequately formulated, the demonstration consists only in making transformations by symbolic substitution. However, problems arise just when we try to state requisites for semantically reliable definitions, since the analysis of characters has to correspond to the analysis of ideas. At the beginning, Leibniz seems to believe that we only need a definition in order to have a distinct idea. However, the finding of contradictory concepts convinces Leibniz later to modify this naïve view and thus he comes to distinguish more rigorously between nominal and real definitions. Whereas the former do not prove the consistency of a concept, the latter do or ought to do that. This view on definition appears initially in the second half of the 1670's and acquires its classical formulation in the *Meditationes*. Independently of these considerations, the semantic aspect of definitions is

However, there are in Leibniz's conception of Symbolic Thought some tensions resulting from the conjunction of features 1 and 2. In fact, the former characterises Symbolic Thought as a purely mechanical procedure that depends only on operation rules strictly and exhaustively formulated, so that it could be carried out by an appropriately devised mechanism, while the latter involves an intentional comprehension of the symbolic expression, since it is characterized as a picture or structural representation of something that is displayed "to the mind" by its means. The fact that Symbolic Thought has a displaying function furnishes to the metaphor of a *filum meditandi* a quality that is not completely expressed by the idea of a mechanical computation, but can be attributed to the notion of visual or diagrammatic reasoning, in which there is some visual comprehension of the operation that is being performed. This comprehension is based on the visual shape of the symbolic arrangement, so that the operation on it is not completely governed by explicit rules. It is unlikely that Leibniz was aware of such a difference between these conflictive perspectives about Symbolic Thought, but it is implicit in the way in which Leibniz characterizes the performances of Symbolic Thought.

Certainly, at different times of his philosophical career, especially since the *Accessio*, Leibniz emphasizes that the fundamental advantage of Symbolic Thought consists in providing us with a physical representation of our thinking by means of symbols or characters. For example, in a letter to Mariotte from July 1676, Leibniz says:

> The human mind cannot advance too far in reasoning without resorting to characters. And characters, when they are adequately chosen, have this marvellous property: they leave so to say marks of our thoughts on paper, and [thus] we provide ourselves with the means of being infallible.[65]

Thus, a character is "...a visible mark that represents thoughts".[66] So, any inferential operation can be expressed visually through a calculation, that is, an operation that uses characters:

> Calculus is nothing more a thing than an operation by means of characters, which takes place not only in quantity, but also in all other reasoning.[67]

---

what introduces specific cognitive content into the formal structures of the Symbolic Thought. See Dascal **1980**, note 27.

[65] A II 1, 269-271.
[66] *De characteribus et de arte characteristica*, ca. 1688, A VI 4, 916.
[67] Letter to Tschirnhaus, May 1678, A II 1, 62. Cfr. the following definition of formal calculus, from some years later: "...Calculus or operation consists in the production of

In the same train of thought, the characterization of calculus as a mechanical procedure that is performed with and on characters qua physical objects appears explicitly in a letter to Oldenburg, a few years earlier. In explaining the advantages of the Characteristic, Leibniz affirms:

> ...this criterion... that makes truth visible and fixed and, so to say, irresistible in a mechanical way... gives as a result that we cannot make mistakes and that the truth is discovered as if it is depicted or as if it has been expressed on paper with the help of a machine.[68]

Thus, the calculus as an operation with characters gives us a mechanical thread for directing our thinking in every reasoning:

> I call thread of meditation a certain guide for the mind, perceptible and quasi-mechanical, which the clumsiest man would acknowledge.[69]

Associated to this view of calculus as a mechanical guide for our reasoning, Leibniz introduces the notion of proof of formal correctness or formal validity, which must be carried out on the symbolic expressions as such, and what is more, such proof is also an algorithmic procedure:

> I have remarked that the reason that we make mistakes so easily outside mathematics and that geometers have been so successful lies in the fact that in geometry as much as in other parts of abstract mathematics continuous experiences or proofs can be carried out not only on the conclusion, but also at every moment and in every step that is performed on the premises, by reducing the whole to numbers... The only means of ordering our reasonings is to make them as perceptible as are the reasonings of the mathematicians, so that one can find their mistakes before one's very eyes; in this way, when there is a

---

relations, which is accomplished by transformations of formulae, which in turn are carried out according to certain prescribed rules." *Fundamenta calculi ratiocinatoris*, ca. 1688, A VI 4, 921.
[68] Letter to Oldenburg, December 1675, A II 1, 393.
[69] Letter to Oldenburg, 1673-1676, A II 1, 379. Cfr. *Analysis linguarum*, 1678, A VI 4, 102: "Therefore, we can make perceptible the analysis of thoughts and direct it as if with a mechanical thread, because the analysis of characters is perceptible... then our understanding must be governed by some kind of mechanical thread, because of its clumsiness."

> controversy among people, one could say only "let's count" without further ceremony, in order to determine who is right.[70]

The concept of Symbolic Thought as a mechanical calculus and the very idea of algorithmic proofs of formal correctness entails the need of a thoroughly formalization of inferential processes in such a way that the handling with symbolic expressions is explicitly and completely governed by the laws of the symbolic system to which these expressions pertain. Thus, inference must be executed by strictly following explicit rules in every step. In this way, Leibniz forges the notion of a thoroughly formalized system,[71] which he calls sometimes Characteristic or calculus:

> Every Characteristic consists in the formation of an expression and in the passage from one expression to another. An expression is simple or composed. The latter is formed either by addition or fusion. Addition results in a formula, whereas by fusion we obtain a new *character*... The passage from an expression to another signifies that if an expression is set, another can also be set. Therefore, it follows that there are formulae that involve or state a passage and also that there are passages from one statement to another statement...[72]

Therefore, it is not surprising that this train of ideas culminates in a view that sees inferential thinking as a quasi-computational process that is performed in terms of a reciprocal substitution of characters:

> Our reasoning is as a whole no more than a connection and substitution of characters, be these characters words, notes or finally pictures. Every substitution, then, results from an equipollence. Furthermore, for this reason it becomes apparent that every reasoning is a combination of characters.[73]

If, as Leibniz seems to suggest, we understand calculus as a completely formalizable and strictly computable procedure, Symbolic Thought is no

---

[70] *Projet et essais pour avancer l'art d'inventer*, 1688-1690, A VI 4, 964. See *La vraie methode*, 1677, A VI 4, 4-6.
[71] Marciszweski **1997**, p 41.
[72] *De characteristica sive calculo*, ca. 1688, A VI 4, 917.
[73] A VI 4, 922, ca. 1688-1690. See also *Fundamenta calculi ratiocinatoris*, 1688, A VI 4, 918 (note 66).

more than a completely regulated operation with characters that does not leave room for any possibility of any kind of intuitive comprehension of inferential steps, and does not require it, because every inferential step is reduced to a regulated transformation of a set of formulae into another formulae. Thus, we obtain a formulation of Symbolic Thought in terms of the ideal of automatic computation. According to this line of argumentation, we arrive at a kind of Symbolic Thought in a strict sense, that is, a completely blind Thought.

The issue is to determine whether Leibniz really conceives of calculus in this formal sense as a powerful aid for our informal thinking or, beyond this, he sees Symbolic Thought as the way in which our understanding works. The former is beyond all doubt the case, as becomes apparent through the metaphor of the *filum meditandi*. The latter, which would convert the human mind into a mere symbolic processor, seems to be more doubtful, despite some Leibnizian claims on behalf of it. In other words, there are forms of Symbolic Thought that do not require the thorough formalization of the symbolic process and that, for this reason, cannot be conceived of as calculus in the strict sense of the word.

In addition, as long as these kinds of Symbolic Thought involve inferential steps that are not strictly regulated, they require some intuitive comprehension.[74] Such intuitivity does not refer to contents or ideas, since we are dealing with Symbolic Thought, but to a certain comprehension of the form or structure of the issue, which is displayed through the symbolic configuration. As a result, the visual appearance of it furnishes a guide for making inferences, although the operations are not completely expressed by formal rules. Therefore, we get a sort of Symbolic Thought that performs its task through a kind of visual reasoning. If this is so, the symbolic form (whatever its nature may be, whether characters, figures or drawings) is not only a physical object, but also is recognised as an image or diagram that represents something.

Thus, we find a class of blind operation *lato sensu* (but not completely blind) that implies a comprehensive vision of structural nature. Furthermore, this form of Symbolic Thought does not exclude the possibility of applying a calculus in the sense of completely blind Symbolic Thought, since the former can be combined with the latter or, even, the procedures of the former can be made explicit in terms of a rigorous calculus. Whatever the case, this alternative view of Symbolic Thought that highlights its diagrammatic aspects makes its displaying function more understandable.

The need to introduce a wide concept of Symbolic Thought arises from two considerations. The first looks at the displaying feature of symbolic configurations that have just been mentioned. For example, the formula is not only a physical entity, but also exposes or displays something before our

---

[74] We use the term 'intuitive' in the sense of 'not formalized', but not in the technical Leibnizian sense.

eyes. The second tries to account for the fact that Leibniz includes in his reflections on the importance of signs and characters for our thinking semiotic systems that cannot be considered as calculi in the strict sense of the word.[75] Examples of that are his allegations on the usefulness of pictures and diagrams (among which Leibniz also includes tabulations) in the inferential procedures, since they also in their way provide a guide for our intellectual tasks. Although they are not subjected to explicit rules of operation, they make manifest structural relations that are not apparent by themselves. At the same time, their visual properties open the possibility for cognitive operations. Finally, if we connect the displaying feature of the formulae with the importance of diagrams, a formula could be conceived of as an extension of the function of pictures and diagrams. Thus, the formula would be a *filum meditandi*, but its advantage would not rest exclusively on its computational performance.

As we have seen, the advantage of characters and formulae consists in the fact that they "paint" or "draw" our thoughts visually on paper. For Leibniz, this painting or drawing involves a certain projection of the structure of that which is represented onto the symbolic form that represents it, so that the syntactical configuration of the formulae corresponds through a relation of structural similarity to the form of the state of affairs represented. Thus, the types of connection among the components of the symbolic expression maintain a correspondence relation with the connections of the structural elements of the object that is represented by this expression. In this way, the formula "makes visible" any structure by means of notation. Occasionally, Leibniz describes as "ecthetic" this kind of analytic representation. Thus, the benefit of an ecthetic representation consists in the fact that it enables, by means of an analytic notation, the schematic representation of the operation laws which the formal connections of the elements of a given object can be subjected to. [76] Leibniz opposes this kind of representation to the merely linguistic or verbal enunciation of the same formal properties, which resort to words, that is, to Verbal Thought, and to the comprehension of "general meanings" but not to schematic notations. Thus, the ecthetic representation, that in fact is a kind of writing, is the most adapted to algorithmic operations, one of the main features of Symbolic Thought:

> From the different ways of combining, where the terms behave similarly or dissimilarly, result universal names that denote relations, that is, conventional terms by means of which, therefore,

---

[75] Generally, we introduce the concept of semiotic system for referring to sign systems not necessarily provided with algorithmic features, whereas we use 'symbolic systems' as signifying 'sign systems with the form of a calculus'.

[76] We take here 'object' in the most general meaning of the word, not restricted only to physical things.

can be expressed universally that which is expressed ecthetically through characters.[77]

This use of "ecthetic" as applied to formulae is not very frequent in Leibniz's writings, although he uses it at least once again in a letter to Burnett from 1699.[78] Anyway, the way in which Leibniz uses the term, traditionally associated to proof procedures both in logic and mathematics, seems to be influenced by the meaning that Jungius gives to the same concept when he is explaining the advantages of symbolic notations.

The term "ecthetic" comes from the Greek word *ékthesis*, which means literally "exposition" or "presentation". It refers to two kinds of method of proof. The first, of a logical nature, is Aristotle's method consisting in the introduction of an individual term for proving inferences.[79] The latter is one of the steps in the Euclidian method for geometric demonstrations. Thus, the *ékthesis* is the presentation in a geometric construction of the data stated in the geometric proposition (*prótasis*), in order to proceed to the demonstration (*apódeixis*) through the addition of supplementary constructions (*kataskéue*). However, in the *Analysis didactica*, a work which Leibniz excerpted abundantly, Jungius uses the term with a meaning that deviates both from the logical and geometric uses, although there is some connection with the latter.

Indeed, following an analogy with the mathematical procedure, Jungius suggests that syllogistic demonstrations can be replaced by a kind of demonstration that he calls ecthetic and that he defines in this way:

> ...however, I call ecthetic demonstration not that one that concludes by using an individual mid term a singularly particular conclusion [with] "some", but that one that puts singularly all of the terms among which are given the relations, so that, however, these relations are not restricted to any matter nor are they limited in their non-material differences more narrowly than it is proposed in the proposition...[80]

In a quite obscure way, Jungius presents here a procedure for symbolically representing the logical form of a proposition. Its diverse components are represented through the assignation of corresponding characters, whose syntax exposes the formal connections that there are among the components of the formalized proposition. The visible nature of

---

[77] *De modis combinandi characteres*, ca. 1688-1699, A VI 4, 923.
[78] Letter to Burnett, 1699, GP 3, 258.
[79] See *Anal. Prior.*, 25ª15; 28ª23 y 28b14. See too Lukasiewicz: **1977**, p. 57-62.
[80] *Analysis didactica*, VE 7, 1629.

the notation gives an analogy of the geometric *ékthesis* and perhaps for this reason Jungius chooses this traditional term. However, such a formalization of a proposition does not furnishes an instantiation, as it is the case in the geometric *ékthesis*, but displays a logical form that can be common to many different propositions.[81] Indeed, Jungius' views on symbolization are accomplished in his essays for introducing symbolic notations, which he calls *Signatoria* and are a forerunner of the Leibnizian *Characteristica*.[82]

The concept of the formula as a special kind of *ékthesis* or "exposition" is another way of presenting the display function of Symbolic Thought which we have talked about previously. From the fact that the syntax of formulae makes a form or structure ostensible it follows that formulae have an ambivalent trait, since on the one hand they are suitable for mechanical computation and on the other they are displaying something that goes beyond themselves. Furthermore, Leibniz sees in this "expositive" capability of formulae the grounds for their performance in invention or discovery, because they make us discover relations or connections that otherwise would be hidden to us, a feature that we could call "expressivity" in speaking of formulae. For this reason, formulae share some features with pictures and diagrams, which also play a role as perceptible guides for thinking, although not necessarily in a mechanical fashion, as we have seen before. As Leibniz says in an essay on universal mathematics:

> The method of invention consists in some thread for thinking, that is, a rule for passing from one thought to another. Indeed, since our mind uses images of perceptible things, one can conclude that if images are linked like a chain, he who carries out the action of thinking could not deviate, whenever he maintains himself attentive... in order to think correctly we need some perceptible instruments that I reduce to two main items, *characters* and *tables*... I call character all that represents another thing to he who carries out the thinking.[83]

What is required from the thread for thinking is only that it helps us to link our thoughts by means of surrogates that are provided by images. On the contrary, calculus as rigorously algorithmic symbolism is not a *sine qua non* condition for Symbolic Thought. For this reason, scale models, pictures and diagrams can also fulfil an important task in directing our inferences,

---

[81] *Ibidem*: "...geometers take the term "ecthesis" in a different sense, by exposing at the beginning of a demonstration the data of a problem, that is, as if they would exhibit them in the very fact and show them in an example."

[82] *Analysis didactica*, VE 7, 1630-1634. See Kangro **1969**.

[83] A VI 4, 324.

especially because we can view them as many species of characters.[84] For example, through a tabular disposition we can find easily that the series of the squares can be obtained by means of the addition of the series of triangular numbers:[85]

0   1   3   6   10   15

1   4   9   16   25

Even though in this table arithmetical calculus is required, the visual disposition of the numerical series constitutes a perceptible element that, literally, guides the inferential process that leads us to the discovery of the next term in the numerical series. In Leibniz's writings there are many examples of tables that facilitate the discovery of mathematical or formal properties. In the field of logic, we can point out the essays of linear representation of the categorical propositions and syllogisms.[86]

However, models and pictures are imperfect ways of representing, because they are often incapable of representing the structural components of the modelled or depicted object in a sufficiently thorough way to make apparent formal connections that can be of significance for determining its structural properties. In other words, the resources of models and pictures are limited in expressivity. Moreover, some objects are far beyond their reach, as happens in geometry, where we cannot represent supersolids through a picture or drawing.[87] For these cases, the formula, as an analytical expression for a set of connections and relations, overcomes the lack of images and diagrams and, at the same time, is an extension of the effectiveness of the former:

> It is necessary to reduce all sciences to pictures and formulae. Certainly, since many things cannot be expressed by pictures... at least they could be

---

[84] A VI 4, 325. "...both models and pictures could be included into the characters..." See too *Fundamenta calculi ratiocinatoris*, A VI 4, 918-919, *Dialogus*, A VI 4, 23 and GM 4, 481.
[85] A VI, 4, 325. See A VI 4, 81. On the usefulness of tables, A VI 4, 416.
[86] See *Generales inquisitiones de analysi notionum et veritatum*, 1686, A VI 4, 771-773 and *De formae logicae comprobatione per linearum ductus*, C 292-321. Concerning the effectiveness of diagrams, see *Characteristica*, ca. 1679, A VI 4, 160: "As well as a philosophical language could be expressed by means of numbers, that is, of arithmetic, a philosophical writing could be exhibited by drawing lines, that is, by means of geometry. Thus, all problems and theorems of the sciences would become no more than theorems of arithmetic or of geometry, with whose aid could be signified the rest of the things."
[87] A VI 4, 326.

subjected to formulae, which play the role of
pictures and serve to fasten the imagination.[88]

The formula as a syntactical construction has a double *status*, so to say.[89] Its ecthetic nature confers to it the function of an image, whereas its regulated syntax allows operations of algorithmic transformations. Its capability of analytical representation allows it to be free of the need of an external similarity, as happens with geometrical figures, or of supplying the lack of explicit syntactical rules through a non-formalized operation, as is the case of tables or diagrams. Thus, the formula makes possible the application of progressive formalizing processes, which are achieved with the explicit enunciation of syntactical rules that govern the handling of formulae. Thus, in a thorough formalization, operation with formulae is directed by the application of syntactical rules of construction and transformation of symbolic expressions. Consequently, we get along with the accomplishment of a complete formalization a purely mechanical calculus, in which nothing at all depends on a not-formalized operation. As a result of such formalization, calculus becomes progressively freer of the consideration of meanings, even of those that have a formal nature, such as the arithmetical or logical relations and operations. Notwithstanding, the formalizing process has to be accompanied by the explicit formulation of rules for assigning meanings to the formal expressions.

Certainly, it is in no way clear that Leibniz keeps in mind the referred distinction between the aforementioned kinds of Symbolic Thought, the comprehensive and the mechanical ones. However, since according to Leibniz's view formulae always express an objective structure or form, a connection of relations, it seems natural to conclude that for him a syntax is not restricted to be a mere notation devoid of any meaning, but also reveals or displays a more or less ideal structure, that can be dealt with in a computational way.

Anyway, Leibniz is fully aware of the potential of a thorough formalization for Symbolic Thought by means of calculi provided with a formal syntax. Indeed, his continuous efforts for constructing conceptual calculi not only are a clear testimony of that,[90] but in addition his permanent search for appropriated notations for the different sciences has to be included in this orientation of his methodological and epistemological investigations. Thus, Leibniz's view on formalization appears with its full significance in the program of the *Characteristica geometrica*,[91] the aim of which is the construction of a calculus of positions as a substitution for the classical dealing with geometrical figures and even for the analytical geometry of

---

[88] A VI 4, 439. See A VI 4, 326.
[89] See *Fundamenta calculi ratiocinatoris*, A VI 4, 920.
[90] See *Generales inquisitiones de analysi notionum et veritatum*, n. 86.
[91] See GM 1, 20-25; GM 5, 141-211; C 548-556 and Leibniz: 1995.

Descartes. Furthermore, as a generalization of his views on formalization, Leibniz conceives of a *Characteristica Generalis*, also named *Combinatoria Characteristica*, which can be characterized as the science of the construction of formal systems in general:

> ...The Combinatory deals with calculus in general, that is, with universal characters or notations, as well as with different laws concerning their disposition and processing, that is, it deals with formulae in general.[92]

The program of this science fully expresses the Leibnizian trend towards complete formalization, since it investigates the languages of the sciences by considering them as reducible to syntactical systems.[93] Thus, syntactical systems are examined with total independence of semantic considerations, which are the object of a separate investigation. Furthermore, motivated by this syntactical approach, Leibniz sees the possibility of giving to the same formal system many different interpretations. As we shall see, following this path we can conclude that the General Characteristic can be viewed as the most accomplished realization of the structural nature of symbolic knowledge, a concept whose meaning is captured by the very idea of Symbolic Thought.

In conclusion, Leibniz's concept of Symbolic Thought (and thus of symbolic knowledge) can be understood as a continuum that goes from the more intuitive forms of use of signs or characters, such as geometric figures,[94] to the most abstract and formal treatments of symbolical systems, such as they are exemplified in the program of the General Characteristic.

4. Surrogation and expression. The structural nature of symbolic knowledge

From now on we will use the term "symbolic knowledge" understanding by it the kind of cognitive representation that is involved in Symbolic Thought; for this reason we will talk about symbolic knowledge as plainly equivalent to Symbolic Thought.

Certainly, knowledge of structures and surrogation was referred to many times in our previous analysis about Symbolic Thought. It is the moment for deepening our analysis of both characteristics of Symbolic Thought and, therefore, of symbolic knowledge. Certainly, surrogation and structural

---

[92] *De artis combinatoria usu in scientia generali*, ca. 1683, A VI 4, 511. See also *De modis combinandi characteres*, 1688-1689?, A VI 4, 921-922.

[93] The outlines of such a reduction can be found in *Fundamenta calculi ratiocinatoris*, A VI 4, 917-922. On *General Characteristic* as distinguished from *Universal Characteristic*, cfr. note 121.

[94] Figures and images are also signs or 'characters'. GM 4, 81: "...however, other sorts of signs are required, among which I include images and words."

nature are tightly tied to each other in Leibniz's view. Both of them are grounded in an incipient theory of structural representation, the core of which is the concept of expression, that is, a kind of projection of the structure of an object into another structure. Expression, a notion akin to the idea of mapping or morphism, becomes thus a key to the cognitive effectiveness of symbolic systems, since it ensures that the formal properties of the object represented are captured by the symbolic connections and operations.

The surrogative function of Symbolic Thought allows us to think or to reason about any objects without having to direct our mind to the contemplation of the very ideas of them. For this reason, we have to spell out some aspects of Leibniz's view on the role of ideas, although we do not intend to exhaust the issue, as its scope exceeds the range of our present analysis.

Indeed, our knowledge of things is always mediated by ideas, which refer to them. Therefore, ideas are the immediate objects of our mind, so that they themselves fulfil a surrogative function, since they represent to us objects that we know indirectly by their means.[95] In turn, signs or characters replace or surrogate ideas. Now, ideas themselves raise a cognitive problem, because, as we have seen before, Leibniz tends to believe that thinking is essentially dependent on some kind of perceptible support; in other words, there is not any thinking that is completely a-symbolic:

> In our imagination there is always something that corresponds to ideas, even if we are dealing with immaterial things, namely characters like those of arithmetic, algebra and words.[96]

Although Leibniz hesitates sometimes on this point, particularly when he is approaching the question of intuitive knowledge,[97] the necessary tie between sign and idea receives a progressive confirmation from the consolidation of the doctrine of the pre-established harmony.[98] Therefore, if there is no idea that is not bound to some kind of sign or symbol, how can we say that symbol systems play a surrogative role or represent ideas? In

---

[95] Concerning this issue, Leibniz introduces a distinction between an idea and notion or concept. While an idea is an active power or faculty of representing, a concept or notion is an actual representation that results from that active power. See *Quid sit idea*, A VI 4, 1370-1371 and *Disocurs de métaphysique*, A VI 4, 1569, 70, 72. An analysis of this point can be found in Poser **1979**, Burkhardt **1980**. See also Dascal **1987**. For an analysis of the concept of idea in the philosophy of 17th Century, see Jolley **1990**.
[96] Letter to Jaquelot, GP 3, 466. See *Dialogus*, 1677, A VI 4, 22. Dascal **1987**.
[97] See *Meditationes de cognitione, veritate et ideiis*, A VI 4, 588; *Discours de métaphysique*, A VI 4, 1568.
[98] *Nouveaux Essais*, A VI 6, 77. See Dascal **1987**. Dascal argues that Leibniz could give a clear-cut solution to the issue of the connection between sign and thought with the introduction of the doctrine of the preestablished harmony, see especially p. 57.

fact, all we have, finally, is a variety of semiotic systems, whereas ideas as such seem to be absent. We consider the answer to this problem can be found in Leibniz's conception of expression. In drawing up this concept, Leibniz took inspiration from projective geometry, although his view has as background epistemological and metaphysical influences that can be traced back to the neoplatonic tradition. Summing up, the answer can be formulated in the following way: symbolic systems not only express ideas (or systems of ideas), but also have the power of reciprocally expressing each other. Since ideas do not appear by themselves, but only through signs, the surrogative function of symbolic systems is accomplished in the correspondence that can be established among the different systems of representation of the same ideas (or system of ideas).

Concerning surrogation, we assume the concept of surrogative reasoning formulated by Chris Swoyer. According to Swoyer, for there to be a surrogative reasoning there has to be an object (in the general meaning of the word) and a structural representation of it. Thus, surrogative reasoning is an inference made on the structural representation in order to draw conclusions about the object represented by it.[99] In Leibniz, the concept of representation matches the features that Swoyer claims for surrogative reasoning. Moreover, symbolic systems are explicitly introduced in Leibniz's definition of representation:

> I call *character* whatever represents another thing for whoever carries out the thinking. It is said that a thing *represents* if it corresponds [to another thing] so that from the former one can know the latter, although they are not similar, as long as all the things that happen in one of them are referred to certain things corresponding to them in the other, according to a rule or some relation. Indeed, for representing likeness is not required, and this is evident from the [example] of the ellipse, which is the projection of the circle in a chart and represents it to the viewer in a very different manner, part by part, although ellipse is not and should not be similar to it. Moreover, what class of similarity can we conceive of between arithmetic characters and numbers or repetition of unities? However, the characters that we use represent numbers in such an accurate way that properties of numbers are discovered by means of characters.[100]

---

[99] Swoyer **1991**, p. 449.
[100] A VI 4, 324. See *Characteristica geometrica*, 1679, GM 5, 141: "Consequently, to every operation that is carried out in characters corresponds an enunciation in things and often we

The coincidences between surrogative reasoning and Leibniz's notion of representation are apparent. The geometrical example of the ellipse accentuates the idea of projection, whereas the arithmetic example shows clearly that for representation there is a need for an operation in the system representing an object whose outcome is transferred then to the object represented by it by virtue of correspondence relations between both of them. Thus, Leibniz states in an informal way the notion of preservation of a structure or order, which is characteristic of the concept of morphism.

As we have pointed out previously, the justification for the representation function is given by Leibniz's concept of expression. Its classical formulation can be found in the essay *Quid sit idea*, from 1678:

> It is said that one thing expresses another when the first contains relations that are in correspondence with the relations of the thing to be expressed.[101]

Thus, the expression is characterized as a projective transformation that preserves structural features, so that it ensures a correspondence between the relations of the object representing on one hand and those of the object represented on the other. Leibniz's characterization of expression is close to the notion of isomorphism, for which an extrinsic or external likeness is not necessary, although it is not excluded.[102] Thus, the structural projection assures the conclusion about structural properties of the object represented from structural features of the object representing it. For this reason, we might say that Leibniz applies a transference principle that would correspond informally to a "representation theorem".[103]

One of the most relevant applications of the transference principle happens in the surrogative reasoning that we carry out with the aid of symbolic representations of any kind:

> But there are various kinds of expression; for example, the model of a machine expresses the machine itself, the projective delineation on a plane expresses the solid, speech expresses thoughts and truths, characters express numbers,

---

can postpone the consideration of things themselves until the outcome of the treatment. Indeed, once one has found in the characters what was looking for, it is easy to find the same in the things by means of what was supposed in the things and through the concordance of the characters."

[101] A VI 4, 1370 [Loemker 206, slightly modified].

[102] Swoyer **1995**, p 81-82. However, there are applications of the expression concept that do not correspond to isomorphism concept. For example, in language there are many names for a same thing. Although concept of isomorphism is an adequate approximation to Leibniz's concept of expression, morphism concept would be perhaps more suitable for accounting Leibniz's concept. For a discussion of recent interpretations of the concept, see Kulstad **2006**.

[103] See Swoyer **1995**, note 18, p 83. For the idea of 'transference', see *Thodicée*, GP 7, 326-327.

and an algebraic equation expresses a circle or some other figure. What is common to all these expressions is that we can pass from a consideration of the relations in the expression to a knowledge of the corresponding properties of the thing expressed.[104]

Thus, semiotic systems are a paradigmatic case of expression. The fundamental condition for that is that there is a correspondence between the sign structure and the object structure represented by the sign. However, such structural correspondence has different degrees of accuracy, depending on the kind of sign or character that we are dealing with. For example, expression can be based in an external and perceptible likeness, as happens with the geometrical figures.[105] But perceptible likeness is not a *sine qua non* condition for expression, since what is needed for an expression relation is only the existence of projection relations preserving structure. Certainly, the object expressed and the expressing object may be completely dissimilar concerning their external and perceptible shape, whenever order relations and operations that take place in one of them can be transformed in the corresponding order relations and operations in the other. Precisely that is what happens with conventional signs of the language or of mathematical notations.[106] Therefore, it may be conclude that there are signs that express (and thus represent) in a natural way because of a perceptible similarity, whereas others signs do it by means of a more complex relation of structural correspondence in which are combined conventional and non-conventional factors.

Leibniz deals with this issue in an essay titled *Dialogus*, from 1677. Here Leibniz examines Hobbes' conventionalist theory of truth: since truth depends on definitions of word meanings, and definitions are conventional, truth is also conventional.[107] Again, definitions are conventional, because they state an equivalence between names imposed conventionally. It is not our present concern to evaluate the objections raised by Leibniz against Hobbes' view. Certainly, the conventionality of a definition is not exactly the same as the conventionality of the names that are part of the definition as a linguistic expression. On the contrary, we are interested in pointing out that Leibniz's solution to the issued proposed by Hobbes resorts to the concept of structural projection, which, as we have seen, is the very core of the Leibnizian notion of expression. Leibniz's argument starts from the surrogative function of the semiotic systems in general. Thus, for example, we can use geometrical figures as surrogates for the corresponding objects in

---

[104] A VI 4, 1370 [Loemker, 206].
[105] A VI 4, 1371 and A VI 4, 23.
[106] A VI 4, 1371.
[107] *Dialogus*, 1677, A VI 4, 22-23 [Loemker 183].

our geometrical reasonings, because they hold a similarity relation with them.[108] Nevertheless, other kinds of signs or characters have no similarity (at least external similarity) with what they represent or surrogate, since they are imposed by convention. In spite of that, they enable successful surrogative inferences.[109] The basis for that is given by the correspondence that exists between the syntax of the symbolic expressions (for example, the formulae of algebra) and the relations and connections that determine the form of the object that they represent. Thus, although characters are conventional, if a notation or language is devised with enough perspicuity, composition and transformation laws for characters and formulae have to correspond both to the structural relations of the object and to the transformation operations that can be applied to it. Again, syntactical components of a symbolic expression are a structural projection or mapping of the object:

> Yet I notice that, if characters can be used for reasoning, there is in them a kind of complex mutual relation or order which fits the things; if not in the single words, at least in their combination and inflection... For although characters are arbitrary, their use and connection have something which is not arbitrary, namely a definite analogy between characters and things...[110]

Therefore, if a projection relation holds between the formula and the object represented by it, it can be concluded that there is also an expression relation between them. Thus, it can be concluded also that different symbolic systems can be expressed reciprocally by each other. Indeed, if each of them express, in spite of their diversity, adequately by means of their respective syntaxes the same object, they will be structure preserving and, for this reason, relations of reciprocal projection or expression can be established among them:

> Their use and connection [of characters] have something which is not arbitrary, namely, a definite analogy between characters and things, and the relations which different characters expressing the same thing have to each other. This analogy or relation is the basis of truth. For the result is that whether we apply one set of characters or another, the products will be the same

---

[108] A VI 4, 23 [Loemker, *ibidem*].
[109] A VI,4, 23-24 [Loemker, *ibidem*].
[110] *Ibidem* [Loemker *ibidem*].

> or equivalent or correspond analogously... And the analytic or arithmetical calculus confirms this view. For in numbers the problem always works out in the same way whether you use the decimal system or as some mathematician did, the duodecimal. Afterward, if you apply the solution you have reached by calculation in several different ways, by arranging kernels or some other countable objects, the answer always comes out the same. In analysis as well, even though different properties of the subject are more easily apparent when different characters are used, the basis of truth is always found in the connection and coordination of these characters.[111]

In fact, Leibniz seems to apply to symbolic systems the transference principle which we have referred to previously. Expression preserves structure and for this reason, if two or more symbolic systems express the same object, we can pass from the one to the other by applying the required transformations. Thus, the outcomes that are obtained by symbolic operations in a determined system can be transformed into the corresponding outcomes of the other, when they express the same thing. The examples preferred by Leibniz are both the numerical systems with different bases and the projective properties of the conics, as well as the correspondences between algebraic equations and geometrical constructions. For this reason Leibniz's conclusion about truth can be restated as follows: the possibility of truth is based in the structural invariance in transformations among symbolic systems or, briefly, truth is what remains as an invariant.

Moreover, the more expressive a symbolic system is, the more perfect it will be. Again, how expressive a symbolic systems is depends on the accuracy with which the structure of the object is mapped onto the syntax of the symbolic system that represents it, since thus operations in the symbolic systems disclose surrogatively structural connections involved in other more evident formal properties of the object.[112] We have already referred to this trait of Symbolic Thought as its "expressivity". As an example of that, the Latin numeration system is less expressive and also less perfect than the Arabic one, and the decimal system is less expressive than the binary one:

> ...Indeed, we calculate much more easily with arithmetical characters than with the roman ones, either with the aid of a pen or in our minds,

---

[111] *Ibidem* [Loemker, *ibidem*].
[112] *Characteristica geometrica*, 1679, GM 5, 141: "the more accurate the characters are, that is, the more relations of things they exhibit, the more useful they will be".

> undoubtedly because Arabic characters are more suitable, that is, they express better the genesis of the numbers.[113]
>
> And it must be acknowledged that the more *autarkeîs* they are the more perfect they become, so that every consequence can be drawn from them. For example, the characteristic of binary numbers is more perfect than the decimal one or than any other, since in the binary characteristic everything that can be affirmed regarding numbers can be demonstrated through its characters, and that does not happen with decimal numbers.[114]

After having examined Leibniz's notion of expression as a kind of structural representation, we would like to return to our initial question about the connections between ideas on one hand and symbolic systems on the other. If we remember our initial questioning, we were arguing that it is not so easy to understand how the correspondence between ideas and their symbolic expression is established, because an idea cannot be conceived as if it were a thing that can be compared with another thing.

Indeed, for Leibniz, expression is a transitive relation. Consequently, if objects are expressed by ideas, as we have seen, and in turn ideas are expressed by symbolic systems, it is natural to conclude that symbolic systems express and also represent objects. For this reason, Leibniz sometimes passes over the relationship between symbols or characters and objects and refers directly to the relationship between ideas and symbolic expressions. More specifically, this relationship is presented by him as a kind of isomorphism, as it was said before:

> I call *character* a visible mark that represents thoughts.
> The *Characteristic art* is the art of forming and ordering characters in such a way that they are in correspondence with thoughts, that is, so that they hold among themselves that relation that thoughts maintain between them.
> An *expression* is the aggregate of characters that represents the thing that is expressed.
> The *law of the expressions* is the following: as well as the idea of the thing that has to be expressed is composed of the ideas of other things, the

---

[113] Letter to Tschirnhaus, GM 4, 461.
[114] A VI 4, 800.

expression of the thing has to be composed of the characters that correspond to those other things.[115]

Thus, by supposing that things are represented or expressed by ideas, Leibniz claims that a symbolic expression has to have a composition that matches that of the idea (and its connections, we may add) that it represents or expresses.[116] But we have already alleged that ideas are essentially dependent on some kind of semiotic support. Consequently, since the objects among which the correspondence relation holds have to be present somehow to the mind so that a correspondence relation can be established, it seems to be impossible that we can speak of an expression relation between ideas on one hand and symbolic structures on the other. Moreover, since we know objects through ideas, the whole Leibnizian view on the possibility of symbolic knowledge apparently collapses. A possible answer to this objection could be found perhaps by arguing that at least for some symbolic systems such as geometry, arithmetic and even algebra there can be a clear way of establishing a correspondence, because we have first geometric figures that hold a similarity relationship to things and on this basis a correspondence relationship can then be established between geometric figures on one hand and arithmetical relations on the other. However, the answer falls short of solving our issue, since both the figures themselves and numbers (as a numerical system) are as much semiotic systems as the others. Of course, for objects not subjected to imagination, as in the case of Metaphysics or Ethics, difficulties cannot be overcome in this manner.

Another strategy for solving our perplexities could be to claim that ideas are dispensable. All we need is a structure preserving transformation among the different symbolic systems, which can be understood as models of abstract structures and whose reference to an objective reality is determined in a pragmatic way. Although Leibniz's views on symbolic thought and symbolic knowledge have a model-theoretical flavour, he would not accept an elimination of ideas on behalf of a pragmatic view.

Nevertheless, it is true also that Leibniz gives no clear-cut answer to the issue that we have pointed out. Despite this, it is possible to find a solution to it in the context provided by his metaphysics and epistemology. The key concepts are, again, Leibnizian expression and the expressive conception of ideas, according to which they are not actual contents or concepts, but expressive powers that are permanently active in our minds. As we have just proposed, Leibniz defends this view on ideas in his essay *Quid sit idea* as well as in other later writings. In fact, for Leibniz an idea is an active power of producing actual representations of an object, so that it can be

---

[115] A VI 4, 916.
[116] As pointed out before, ideas are immediate objects of the mind, A VI 4, 1570. See A VI 4, 102: "...the analysis of thoughts corresponds to the analysis of characters that we use for signifying thoughts, since to each character it corresponds a thought".

characterized as an expressive faculty of thinking about an object[116], whereas notions or concepts are the actual outcomes of such expressive power. From this point of view, ideas could be conceived as powers of producing semiotic systems through which they are actually expressed. Certainly, the expressive view on ideas requires the introduction into the nature of the expression of a dynamic-metaphysical aspect that goes far beyond the existence of mere structural correspondences: Ideas deploy in their outcomes the semiotic systems, as the unity in the plurality; however, the explanation of that dynamic deployment is furnished by the projective notion of structural correspondence.

From this point of view, different semiotic systems that are expressions of the same ideas would be isomorphic, because they could be transformed reciprocally into each other. Thus, ideas would not ever manifest themselves by themselves, but only would do so necessarily through a variety of semiotic systems reciprocally expressing each other. Therefore, all that remained to us concerning knowledge would be the internal coherence of each system, the possibility of passing from one system to the others by means of the appropriated transformations and, finally, the successful outcome of our perceptions and actions. In this way, we do not get ideas themselves, but only traces of them; that is, what is captured in the lattice of semiotic systems. Indeed, we do not sustain that Leibniz explicitly states such a thesis, which has a postmodernist flavour, we argue only that our interpretation based on Leibniz's views on expression and ideas could answer our initial question about the relationship between ideas and signs in a way that is consistent with Leibniz's concept of universal harmony and with the perspectivism that it entails.[117]

In conclusion, if ideas express themselves through semiotic systems and what we know of them are actually the systematic interconnectedness of those systems, we would not go astray if we concluded that what we know through the symbolic expressions and their mutual correspondences is the structure generated by the ideas, but not the ideas in themselves. As we have already said, Leibniz is ambiguous about our ability to gain a direct knowledge of ideas, but he claims sometimes that pure and intuitive knowledge is like an ideal whose thorough achievement is hardly attainable by human understanding. Anyway, that ideas express themselves in semiotic systems whose correspondences accentuates the significance of the structures for the cognitive relevance of symbolic systems. Thus, we face a feature of symbolic knowledge to which we have referred many times in our previous analysis: its structural character. We would like now to focus our attention on it.

Certainly, concepts such as 'expression' and 'ecthetic representation', which we have shown to be the basis for the surrogative function of

---

[117] For a structural view on ideas and knowledge, see also Krämer **1991**, whose interpretation is close to ours.

symbolic structures, both disclose its structural roots. Indeed, the weight of their structural import is so determining that Leibniz seems to defend a structural or formalist view of truth. Concerning this question, we have examined earlier the significance that Leibniz attributes to invariance as a preservation of an identical complex of structural relations that are supposed to pertain to the things themselves.[118] Thus, the structural identity makes possible the "morphisms" or "mappings" among different symbolic systems that are used for representing a same kind of objects, so that Leibniz concludes that this invariance system is "...the basis of truth."[119]

However, in spite of the surrogative function of symbolic knowledge, there are some aspects of the Leibnizian concept that go beyond a purely representational view on symbolic knowledge. Sometimes the problem is introduced as an open question to which Leibniz gives no explicit answer. Such is the case, for example, of the infinitesimals,[120] which are frequently conceived by him often as "useful fictions for calculation". Moreover, the same happens with negative and imaginary numbers. However, Leibniz overcomes the representative or surrogative level for his views on symbolic knowledge especially when he outlines his programmatic approaches to his *General Characteristic*, which we have characterized in an earlier section as the science of the construction of thoroughly formalized syntactical calculi. Briefly, the structural nature of symbolic knowledge is made explicit precisely through Leibniz's program for the General Characteristic.

Indeed, Leibniz envisions General Characteristic, called also "Science of forms or formulae" or "Science of the similar and dissimilar", not only as a formal syntax, but also as theory or science that deals with the most general and abstract forms, such as they are exhibited through the general syntactical forms, that is, formulae. General Characteristic has not to be confused with Leibniz's project of creating a universal rational language, to which he sometimes gives the name of *Characteristic* (maybe *Universal Characteristic*), although both projects are tightly intertwined.[121] In fact, whereas Universal Characteristic is a unified language for all of the sciences, General Characteristic aims to become a science about the formal structures that are instantiated in the different sciences, independently of the specific kind of objects that they deal with. Such formal structures can be shared by many sciences and for this reason they constitute invariant forms that remain identical from science to science.[122] Thus, General Characteristic is a syntactical science, devoid of any content. Its object is given in the formal properties of formulae that display general forms of relations, operations and

---

[118] A VI 4, 17.
[119] See note 110.
[120] As for the role played by infinitesimals in symbolic knowledge, see Grosholz **2007**, especially chap. 8, and Serfati **2008**. My views on symbolic knowledge are akin to the interpretation given by Serfati.
[121] For the differences between both projects, see Esquisabel **2002**.
[122] A II 1, 412; A VI 4, 510-512; A VI 4, 545; C 530-531.

connections, without receiving any particular interpretation or meaning.[123] Therefore, it is an abstract science that investigates the laws of composition and transformation of empty forms.[124] Certainly, forms or formulae can acquire a determined meaning, but for that goal they must be interpreted —they must be "applied" in Leibniz's words— into a specific theoretical domain in which the set of formal laws is "satisfied", so that the group of objects pertaining to that domain become, in contemporary terms, a model of the formal system.[125]

Thus, General Characteristic is an abstract science that is two-sided, so to say. One side looks at the syntax of the symbolic construction (General Characteristic as the science of formulae), whereas the other one looks at the form or structure that the symbolic construction displays or exhibit. Thus, forms are shown as syntactic properties of abstract formulae. Consequently, in General Characteristic formulae are liberated from their surrogative function, because they do not stand anymore for an object or a fact, as long as they have no determined and concrete meaning, so that there is nothing that outcomes of syntactical operation can be transferred to. Anyway, abstract formulae fulfil a surrogative function when they receive a particular interpretation in the domain of a specific science. For this reason, General Characteristic is an abstract ecthetic science in the sense that its syntactical expressions exhibit or display the common structures that are partaken by a diversity of theoretical domains. As a conclusion, it could be said that symbolic knowledge not only fulfils in Leibniz's project on the General Characteristic its very essence, that is, to be fundamentally structural knowledge, but also achieves a reflexive or second-order level, since we obtain through such a science a symbolic knowledge of the structural invariants on which the surrogative function of specific symbolic systems is based. Finally, the science of forms is a discipline devoid of any object, unless we acknowledge as its object the very structures as such, which one might say contain the form of a theory in general. Indeed, as long as General Characteristic is a theory about theory structures, we could see in it a science of the conditions of possibility for symbolic knowledge as such.

5. Concluding remarks

In describing the nature and scope of the General Characteristic we have reached the highest point in Leibniz's concept of symbolic knowledge. Lastly, we would like to sum up the main arguments and conclusions of our exposition.

---

[123] A VI 4, 920-922 and 922-923.
[124] GM 7, 24.
[125] A VI 4, 834.

We began with an examination of the concept of symbolic knowledge as Leibniz presents it in the *Meditationes* in order to determine its essential features. Thus, we concluded that Leibniz characterizes symbolic knowledge ambiguously, since it is shown as possessing positive traits as well as negative ones, so that the very notion of symbolic knowledge becomes suspect and doubtful. To overcome these concerns, we had to trace the path of the notion from the *Dissertatio de arte combinatoria* on. Thus, we arrived at the conclusion that both "symbolic thought" and "symbolic knowledge" were denominations used in the *Meditationes* as equivalent to "blind thought". Departing from an analysis of the features of blind thought, we sustained the need to distinguish between two kinds of blind thought: Symbolic Thought and Verbal Thought. The former takes as a paradigm algorithmic symbolic systems such as they are exemplified by arithmetic, algebra and definition systems, whereas the latter is represented by verbal or phonic ordinary languages. Thus, according to our analysis, whereas negative aspects of the use of signs result from resorting to Verbal Thought, the positive ones are based on the nature of Symbolic Thought. At the same time, we have tried to show that both views on blind thought are conflated together without distinction in the *Meditations* and later writings. After having argued that Leibniz sees in the features of Symbolic Thought what furnishes epistemic certainty to the uses of signs, we considered Symbolic Thought as the very elucidation of Leibniz's views on symbolic knowledge. Thus, symbolic knowledge is a kind of knowledge that is obtained by means of Symbolic Thought. In turn, Symbolic Thought, as a thought that depends on the use of formulae and diagrams, is characterized by the following features:[126]

1. Symbolic expressions can be treated as physical systems subjected to operation rules, so that they can be manipulated like other physical objects. Thus, Symbolic Thought corresponds in general to the general notion of calculus or computation. However, Leibniz's attitude to this feature involves some ambiguities depending on the way in which the concept of calculus is understood.

2. Symbolic Thought fulfils a surrogative function corresponding to the concept of surrogative reasoning: the contemplation or consideration of ideas or things is replaced or substituted by our dealing with symbolic expressions. Symbolic surrogation is based on the analytical design of symbolic expression pertaining to symbolic systems that are rule-governed and has the general structure of a calculus. In this way, the structure of the object or state of affairs is projected into the syntax of the symbolic expression. Probably following Jungius, Leibniz describes as "ecthetic expression" the formula resulting from such a projection.

---

[126] Esquisabel & Legris **2003**. See also Krämer **1991** and Krämer **1992**.

Consequently, the surrogative function is grounded in the ecthetic nature of the symbolic arrangement.

3. The cognitive function of Symbolic Thought is mainly based on the possibility of capturing in the syntax of a specific symbolic system the formal structures that determine formally the objective domain represented by it. Leibniz explains this possibility in terms of the notion of expression that has been advanced in point 2 with our reference to a projective procedure. Thus, the concept of expression can be understood in terms of an isomorphism or at least of a morphism between the symbolic system and its corresponding objective domain. Moreover, the structural invariance on which isomorphisms or morphisms are based can become an explicit object of a structural science. Leibniz conceived of the possibility of such a science, calling it General characteristic or the General science of forms or formulae. Thus, symbolic knowledge involves structural knowledge, which is made explicit in the General Characteristic.

4. The distinguishing trait of Symbolic Thought is that symbolic expressions can be detached from their meanings when inferential operations are carried out. Reasoning becomes thus a kind of computation. By means of the same meaning abstraction syntactical and structural knowledge can be also gained. Therefore, the formal properties of symbolic systems can be investigated and examined abstractly and formally. In this way, we obtain formal syntactical systems, whereas the meaning assignment depends on explicitly stated semantic rules. Following this idea, Leibniz admits that the same formal system can admit many different interpretations.

5. Moreover, semiotic systems that fulfil the conditions required by the concept of Symbolic Thought play an instrumental role for our thinking. They are conceived as instruments of reason and as a *filum meditandi*, in the sense that they provide us with a perceptible guide for our inferences, so that the correctness of our inferential steps can be tested directly on the perceptible composition of the symbol formation. Therefore, Symbolic Thought makes possible the application of tests "before our eyes" (*ante oculos, ob oculos*), so that truth is determined metaphorically speaking by means of a kind of empirical evidence. Consequently, Symbolic Thought ensures the highest level of certainty that human intellect can reach.

6. Last but not least, Symbolic Thought carries out a psychotechnic function, in that it simplifies cognitive operations and especially relieves the tasks of our memory. Furthermore, the abbreviation function involves a symbolic constitution, and thus also a structural one.

In conclusion, Leibniz's concept of symbolic knowledge involves concepts that are close to the notion of formal calculus or formal syntax on the one hand, but that highlight the displaying character of symbolic expressions, on the other. For this reason, our analysis has shown that there is an internal tension in Leibniz's views that remains not completely resolved: on the one hand, human thinking is modelled on the paradigm of mechanical computing, on the other, there is a kind of comprehension of the form or structure that is exhibited or displayed by formulae or diagrams, so that the scope of blind thought (completely blind thought) would be restricted. If it is so, we should admit some kind of formal thought or even formal intuition that takes place together with symbolic operations. Leibniz gives few indications in this respect. However, whether Leibniz gives us some hints on this topic or not, the question whether there is a kind of formal intuition or not might constitute a not always visible path through which the issue of the cognitive import of formal systems can be approached, even today. In his way, the ideas put forward by Leibniz represent a good starting-point for its discussion.

References

Baumgarten, Alexander G. 1757. *Metaphysica*, Halle (electronic edition of the 2nd edition 1757 in www.ikp.uni-bonn.de/Kant/agb-metaphysica/auditori-benevolo.html).

Bodemann, Eduard. 1966. *Die Leibniz-Handschriften der Königlichen Öffentlichen Bibliothek zu Hannover*. Mit Ergänzungen und Register von Gisela Krönert und Heinrich Lackmann, sowie einem Vorwort von Karl-Heinz Weimann, Hildesheim, Georg Olms.

Burkhardt, Hans. 1980. *Logik und Semiotik in der Philosophie von Leibniz*. Munich, Philosophia Verlag.

Cajori, Florian. 1928/29. *A History of Mathematical Notations*. La Salle, Open Court Publishing Company. Two volumes [repr. NY, Dover Publications, 1993]

Darjes, Joachim Georg. 1742. *Introductio in Artem inveniendi seu logicam theoretico-practicam, qua analytica atque dialectica in usum et jussu*. Jena.

Dascal, Marcelo. 1978. *La sémiologie de Leibniz*. Paris, Aubier.

Dascal, Marcelo. 1987. "Signs and Thought in Leibniz's *Paris Notes*". In: Marcelo Dascal, *Leibniz. Language, Signs and Thought. A Collection of Essays*. Amsterdam/Philadelphia, John Benjamins Publisching Company, pp. 48-59.

Dascal, Marcelo. 1980. Leibniz's Early View on Definition, *Studia Leibnitiana Supplementa*, 21, vol. III, pp. 33-50.

Esquisabel, Oscar M. & Javier Legris. 2003. "Conocimiento simbólico y representación". In *Representación en ciencia y arte*, ed. by Leticia Minhot & Ana Testa. Córdoba (Argentina), Brujas - Universidad Nacional de Córdoba, pp. 233-243.

Esquisabel, Oscar M. 2002. ¿Lenguaje racional o ciencia de las fórmulas? La pluridimiensionalidad del programa leibniziano de la Característica General". *Manuscrito*, 147-197.

Favaretti Camposampiero, Matteo. 2007. *Filum cogitandi. Leibniz e la conoscenza simbolica*. Introduzione di Luigi Perissinotto, Milano Mimesis Edizioni.

Grosholz, Emily. 2007. *Representation and Productive Ambiguity in Mathematics and the Sciences*. Oxford, Oxford University Press.

Kangro, Hans. 1969. "Joachim Jungius und Gottfried Wilhelm Leibniz. Ein Beitrag zum geistigen Verhältnis beider Gelehrten", *Studia Leibnitiana*, 1, pp. 175-207.

Krämer, Sybille. 1991. *Berechenbare Vernunft. Kalkül und Rationalismus im 17. Jahrhundert*. Berlin, Walter de Gruyter.

Krämer, Sybille. 1992. "Symbolische Erkenntnis bei Leibniz". *Zeitschrift für philosophische Forschung*, vol. 46, pp. 224-237.

Krämer, Sybille. 1997. "Kalküle als Repräsentation. Zur Genese des operativen Symbolismus in der Neuzeit". In: H.-J. Rheinberger, M. Hagner, B. Wahring-Schmidt (eds.), *Räume des Wissens: Repräsentation,Codierung, Spur. Berlin*, Akademier Verlag, pp. 113-122.

Kulstad, Mark. 2006. "Leibniz on Expression: Reflection After Three Decades", in: Herbert Breger, Jürgen Herbst and Sven Erdner (eds.), VIII. Internationaler Leibniz-Kongress. Einheit in der Vielheit. Vorträge 1. Teil, Hannover, pp. 413-419.

Lambert, Johann Heinrich. 1764. *Neues Organon oder Gedanken über die Erforschung und Bezeichnung des Wahren und dessen Unterscheidung von Irrthum und Schein*, vols. 1-2 (reprinted in *Philosophische Schriften*, vols. 1-2) Leipzig.

Lambert, Johann Heinrich. 1965. *Philosophische Schriften*, vols. 1-10 (until now edited vols. 1-4, vols. 6 and 7, vol. 9) edited by Hans-Werner Arndt. Hildesheim, G. Olms Verlag. Leipzig. 1764).

Jolley, Nicholas. 1990. *The Light of the Soul. Theory of Ideas in Leibniz, Malebranche and Descartes*, Oxford, Clarendon Press.

Leibniz, Gottfreid Wilhelm. 1903. *Opuscules et fragments inédits*, ed. by Louis Couturat. Paris (repr. by Georg Olms Verlag, Hildesheim/New York. 1988). Quoted as *C*.

Leibniz, Gottfried Wilhelm Leibniz. 1969. *Philosophical Papers and Letters*, ed. by Leroy E. Loemker. Dordrecht/Boston/London, D. Reidel Publishing Company. Quoted as *Loemker*.

Leibniz, Gottfried Wilhelm. 1843-63. *Mathematische Schriften*, vols. 1-7, edited by C. I. Gerhardt. Berlin und Halle (repr. by Georg Olms Verlag, Hildesheim/New York. 1971). Quoted as *GM* followed by volume and page number.

Leibniz, Gottfried Wilhelm. 1875-1890. *Philosophische Schriften*, vols. 1-7, edited by C. I. Gerhardt. Berlin (repr. by Georg Olms Verlag, Hildesheim/New York. 1978) Quoted as *GP* followed by volume and page number.

Leibniz, Gottfried Wilhelm. 1923. *Sämtliche Schriften und Briefe*, edited by the German Academy of Sciences in Berlin, since 1923. Quoted as *A*, followed by series, volume and page number.

Leibniz, G. W. 1982-1991. *Vorausedition zur Reihe VI –Philosophische Schriften– in der Ausgabe der Akademie der Wissenschaften Berlin*. Bearbeitet von der Leibniz-Forschungsstelle der Universität Münster, 10 Bände, Münster. Quoted as VE.

Łukasiewicz, Jan. 1977. *La silogística de Aristóteles desde el punto de vista de la lógica formal moderna*, trans. from the 2nd. edition by Josefina Fernández Robles and rewied by Manuel Garrido. Madrid, Tecnos.

Maimon, Salomon. 1790. *Versuch über die Transzendentalphilosophie mit einem Anhang über die symbolische Erkenntnis und Anmerkungen*, ed. by Andreas Berger (electronic edition of the edition of 1790 in: http://tiss.zdv.uni-tuebingen)

Marciszewski, Witold. 1997. "Leibniz's Idea of Automated Reasoning Compared with Modern AI". In: Halina Święczkowska (ed.), *On Leibniz's*

Philosophical Legacy. Białystok, The Chair of Logic, Informatics and Philosophy of Science, University of Białystok, pp. 35-53.

Poser, Hans. 1979. "Signum, notion und idea". *Zeitschrift für Semiotik*, pp. 310-324.

Schweiger, Clemens, C. 2001. "Symbolische und intuitive Erkenntnis bei Leibniz, Wolf und Baumgarten", en: Hans Poser (ed.), *Akten des VII. Internationalen Leibniz-Kongress. Nihil sine Ratione. Mensch, Natur und Technik im Wirken von G. W. Leibniz. Berlin, 11.-14. September 2001.* Berlin, Druckhaus Berlin-Mitte pp 1178-1183.

Serfati, Michel. 2005. *La revolution symbolique. La constitution de l'écriture symbolique mathématique*. Paris, Pétra.

Serfati, Michel. 2008. "Symbolic Inventiveness and "Irrationalist" Practices in Leibniz's Mathematics", en: Marcelo Dascal (ed.), *Leibniz: What Kind of Rationalist?* New York/Berlin, Springer, pp. 125-139.

Swoyer, Chris. 1991. "Structural Representation and Surrogative Reasoning". *Synthese*, vol. 87, pp. 449-508.

Swoyer, Chris. 1995. "Leibnizian Expression". *Journal of the History of Philosophy*, pp. 65-99.

Wolff, Christian. 1738. *Psychologia Empirica*, Leipzig und Frankfurt (repr. in *Gesammelte Werke*, 2nd Section, vol. 5).

Wolff, Christian. 1968. *Gesammelte Werke*, ed. by J. Ecole, J. E. Hofmann, M. Thomann, H. W. Arndt, Hildesheim, Georg Olms Verlag.

2

Kantian avatars of symbolic knowledge

The role of symbolic manipulation in Kant's philosophy of mathematics[*]

ABEL LASSALLE CASANAVE

The principal aim of this chapter is to show the role played by symbolic manipulation in Kant's philosophy of mathematics. In section 1, we go over the functions of the signs and symbolism associated with Leibnizian symbolic knowledge. We also recall in this section the disagreement between the Kantian notion of "symbolic knowledge" and the meaning of this expression in the Leibnizian tradition. Kant's interest in the *Critique of Pure Reason* (henceforth *Critique*) was centered on arithmetic and geometry, both linked to the notion of ostensive construction, while relegating algebra and symbolic manipulation to a peripheral place. This stands in sharp contrast to the approach found in the *Inquiry concerning the distinctness of the principles of natural theology and morality* (henceforth *Inquiry*). In section 2, we show in a detailed manner how in the *Inquiry* the surrogating, computational, *ecthetic* and psychotechnic functions of symbolism associated with symbolic knowledge are the grounds for mathematical knowledge - a relevant aspect ignored in the literature. This fact that symbolic manipulation moves from a central place in the *Inquiry* to a peripheral one in the *Critique* is of course part of Kant's transcendental turn. But an important thesis remains unaltered, namely: philosophical problems do not admit *more mathematico* treatment, a topic that will be treated in section 3. Thus, we emphasize that philosophy of mathematics was never an autonomous affair for Kant. Finally, in the very notion of *symbolic* or

---

[*] I would like to thank André Porto (UFG / Brasil), Chr. Klotz (UFG / Brasil), J. Legris (UBA / Argentina), J. J. da Silva (UNESP / Brasil), L. C. Pereira (PUC-RJ / Brasil) and, especially, O. M. Esquisabel (UNLP / Argentina), for many suggestions. Finally, I want to thank P. Mancosu (U.C. at Berkeley / USA) for his helpful commentary to the last version of this paper. This work was supported by the National Council for Scientific and Technological Development (CNPq, Brazil) [306044/2007-2, 475534/2008-5].

characteristic construction we can also recognize, as will be shown in section 4, the heritage of Leibniz's notion of symbolic knowledge in Kant's critical philosophy of mathematics.

1. From Leibniz to Kant

Sensualization of thought was a Leibnizian leitmotiv. For instance, in the *Meditations on Knowledge, Truth, and Ideas*, of 1684,[1] Leibniz states in general that we employ signs in place of things or ideas to obtain knowledge. As Leibniz informs us in an untitled text dated *circa* 1684, the class of *signs* includes "words, letters, as well as chemical, astronomical, Chinese and hieroglyphic figures, and musical, stenographical, arithmetical and algebraic notations, and everything that we use in place of things when we think".[2] He immediately adds that written, drawn or sculpted signs are denominated *characters*. Thus, at first glance, signs or characters perform a *surrogating function*: we replace things or concepts by signs. However, an attentive consideration of the matter shows that this preliminary characterization requires a more elaborated account of the notion of surrogating function.

When knowledge is obtained by direct and simultaneous consideration of the simplest notes compounding a distinct idea, it is *intuitive*, in so far as these simplest notes are intuitively known too. This characterization implies that intuitive knowledge is somewhat difficult to achieve. It can be said that it is merely an ideal kind of knowledge. In general terms, our knowledge (and thought) is symbolic or blind, namely, it is obtained (or realized) by means of signs or characters. According to Leibniz, the paradigmatic realization of symbolic knowledge is found in arithmetic and algebra. The arithmetical and algebraic notations can be treated as physical systems which are subjected to operational rules, that is, as systems associated with a *computational function*. The proper use of such rules can be verified by visual inspection, disregarding the designated entities (*cognitio caeca*), and in so doing, our knowledge reaches *ante oculos* certainty. In the aforementioned untitled text, Leibniz writes:

> Although natural languages are very useful for reasoning, however they are submitted to innumerous mistakes and cannot carry out the function of calculation, namely, to the extent that errors in reasoning can be detected from the very formation and construction of words, as if they

---

[1] A VI 4, 585-592; GP IV, 422-426. Leibniz' philosophical and mathematical works are quoted according to the *Akademie* edition, quoted A, and the corresponding Gerhardt editions, GP and GM respectively. We also use Couturat edition, quoted C.
[2] A VI 4, 918-919; GP VII, 204.

were solecisms and barbarisms. Certainly, only the notations of Arithmeticians and Algebrists, for whom all reasonings consist of the use of characters and a mind's error is the same as an error in calculation, perform until now this admirable benefit.[3]

The symbolic *formulae* of arithmetic and algebra perform an *ecthetic function*: that of *expressing* a designated given idea through syntax, or even that of *constituting* a new one. As it is well known, *ecthesis* is a step of the Euclidean demonstrations that consists of setting out a figure which is connected to the problem to be solved or theorem to be demonstrated. However, the use of the term *ecthetic* by Leibniz seems inspired by the writings of Jungius, who used it in the sense of symbolic representation of concepts by means of signs or characters. Finally, the blind governed manipulation of symbolic expressions also has, according to Leibniz, a *psychotechnic function*, namely, that of the economy of thinking as well as avoiding memory burdening.[4]

The belief that signs actually stand for concepts can be wrong, for example, when the intended concept is contradictory; in this case, there is no knowledge at all. For this reason, Leibniz sometimes used the expression "suppositive knowledge". In arithmetic, the surrogating function of signs is not in question: the idea of a (natural) number comes closest to an instance of a distinct idea of which we also know, distinctively, its components. Every numeral and every functional symbol stands for its corresponding idea; for Leibniz, blind manipulation of these symbols (algorithm) leads to sure knowledge. And here, the economy of thinking is easily grasped: *in principle* one could reach intuitive knowledge, say, even for the sum of large numbers, but that would limit progress in arithmetic. Thus, in arithmetic, symbolic knowledge is a *succedaneum* of intuitive knowledge. Algebra's case is more complex.

There were different views on the nature of algebra in the 17th century. According to one of them, by algebra we understand a method of solving arithmetic, geometric or even physical problems. Let us take, for instance, the Cartesian proposal of illumination of the "obscure art of algebra". Here, algebraic letters stand for line segments and the functional symbols +, −, ×, ÷ and √ stand for the so-called "rational operations" of line segments. This procedure allows Descartes to theoretically ground, simultaneously, the *introduction* of "new geometrical entities (and operations)", beyond Euclidean restrictions, as well as the *exclusion* of others. The corresponding clear and distinct mathematical ideas are formulated by algebraic equations,

---

[3] A VI 4, 919; GP VII, 205. Esquisabel's translation.
[4] For details of all these functions, see chapter 1; see also Esquisabel **1999**.

that is, by equating terms involving only rational operations. One could talk about symbolic knowledge in Descartes: the geometric problem is expressed in algebraic terms and the signs are manipulated in order to find the solution of the equation. Nevertheless, if we understand algebra this way, its autonomy is limited: the roots of the equation must be geometrically found, disregarding the "unreal" solutions (square roots of negatives magnitudes, for example) that result from "mere" algebraic manipulation. Thus, the signs surrogate the corresponding "entities" only *up to a certain extent.*

Of course, the Cartesian notion of intuitive knowledge sets limits to the acceptability of mathematical concepts and methods. On account of mathematical and scientific reasons, such restrictions are unacceptable for Leibniz. Consider, for example, the importance of the introduction of imaginary or infinitesimal magnitudes for mathematics and for physics.[5] Often these magnitudes have similar treatments: such "well-grounded fictions" (Leibniz's term) are thought to be *eliminable*, that is, instruments that allow us to calculate in an abbreviated form (areas by means of infinitesimals, for instance) which could be performed otherwise (e.g., by the exhaustion method). This is a second view on algebra found in the 17th century. These fictions would be called, according to contemporary terminology, *ideal elements*. In other words, *in the strictest sense of the word,* the corresponding signs do not *surrogate*, instead they are instruments of a calculus. In this case, symbolic knowledge is conceived by Leibniz as an *instrumental extension* of intuitive knowledge or previously accepted knowledge. In a letter to Varignon, Leibniz says:

> It follows from this that even if someone refuses to admit infinite and infinitesimal lines in a rigorous metaphysical sense and as real things, he can still

---

[5] Some aspects of Leibniz's criticism to Descartes seem relevant. Leibniz saw an unacceptable obstacle to the development of mathematics in the deficiencies of the Cartesian conception of definition. The same objection could be established from a complementary perspective: we cannot restrict the development of mathematics by exclusively appealing to what is given by intuition. For Leibniz, the exclusive resource to intuition implied a sort of also unacceptable subjectivism: the intuitive instance must be replaced, whenever possible, by the inter-subjective instance of definition *with its corresponding demonstration of the possibility of the definite:* in mathematics, possibility implies existence. For Leibniz, it is not about denying the intuitive instance, but limiting its methodological scope: restricting the range of intuition to simple ideas, that is, to the ideas that cannot be defined by their own nature. For the complex ideas, even for those that could be intuitively accessible, the proper methodological resource is the definition, that is, the introduction of a concept through symbolism. A paradigmatic example of this is found in Leibniz and Descartes' positions regarding π. For Descartes, the relationship between the diameter and circumference cannot be included in geometry: it is an "inexact" relationship that cannot be the object of intuition. On the other hand, Leibniz's definition of $\pi/4 = 1 - 1/3 + 1/5 - 1/7 \dots$ allows a legitimate access to such concept: the infinite can be expressed through a finite number of words. We can observe that the possibility of the definite could be decided mechanically for the mere consideration of characters. See Belaval **1967**; Dascal **1987**.

use them with confidence as ideal concepts which shorten his reasoning, similar to what we call imaginary roots in the ordinary algebra, for example $\sqrt{-2}$.[6]

According to a third view, algebra can be conceived as providing knowledge about relations. Such conception certainly anticipates the modern understanding of algebra developed since the third decade of the 19th century and definitively formulated only in the 20th century. The same view was also anticipated in the 17th century by Leibniz.

In this case, for Leibniz, the function of signs does not seem to be exactly one of surrogation, that is, the *ecthetic* function of formulae does not consist in expressing a designated given idea. What we get to know through symbolism are "forms", "structures" or 'relations": thus, symbolic knowledge acquires a dimension of knowledge of pure forms. We can say that according to this view symbolic knowledge is formal knowledge. In *On Universal Synthesis and Analysis, or the Art of Discovery and Judgment*, Leibniz says:

> Fort the rest, the art of combinations in particular, as I take it (it can also be called a general characteristic or algebra), is that science in which are treated the forms or formulas of things in general, that is, quality in general or similarity and dissimilarity; in the same way that ever new formulas arise from the elements a, b, c themselves when combined with each other, whether these elements represent quantities or something else. This art is distinct from common algebra, which deals with formulas applied to quantity only or to equality and inequality. This algebra is thus subordinate to the art of combinations and constantly uses its rules. But these rules of combination are far more general and find application not only in algebra but in the art of deciphering, in various games, in geometry itself when it is treated linearly in the manner of the ancients, and finally, in all matters involving relations of similarity.[7]

---

[6] GM IV, 91-95 [Loemker **1969**, p. 543].
[7] *De Synthesi et Analysi Universali seu arte inveniendi et judicandi*, A VI 4, 538-54 ; GP VII, 292-298 [Loemker **1969**, p. 233].

Thus, we can recognize three kinds of symbolic knowledge (or, at least, three ways to found it), namely, being a *succedaneum* of intuitive knowledge, *extending instrumentally* intuitive knowledge and being *formal*. They are linked to the following foundational problems raised by "the algebraic mode of thought": a) what algebraic thinking is; b) what algebra is about (objects or relations); and, c) what the ontological commitments associated with the entities introduced by symbolic means are.[8] Aside from this, the algebraic mode of thought also had consequences for the concept of number, that is, the progressive abandonment of an *ontological* concept of number in favor of a *symbolic* one.[9] All these aspects of the algebraic mode of thought will be relevant when we examine the avatars of symbolic knowledge in Kant.[10]

In the 18th century, the use of the expression "symbolic knowledge" as opposed to "intuitive knowledge" was usual in Germany. In *Introductio in Artem Inveniendi*, Daries writes: "That which the soul represents to itself, is perceived by signs or it is not. Therefore, given that to know something is the same as to represent it, our knowledge is either intuitive or symbolic."[11] In *Metaphysica*, Baumgarten states: "If the sign and the designated are jointly understood, and the perception of the sign is greater than that of the designated, then such *knowledge* is *symbolic*; if the perception of the designated is greater than that of the sign, then *knowledge* will be *intuitive*."[12] According to Daries, the simple perception without signs is intuitive knowledge; according to Baumgarten, the distinction refers to the attention given to either the sign or the designated. In *Psychologia Empirica*, Wolff seems to be closer to Leibniz when he says that "intuitive knowledge is distinct knowledge"[13] and "very difficult"[14] to achieve. Later, he adds that if "we do not intuit the ideas invoked by words or signs then knowledge is symbolic."[15]

As for Kant, he never used the expression "symbolic knowledge" in the Leibnizian sense. In the 1770's *Dissertation*, Kant defined the knowledge "of what belongs to the understanding"[16] as symbolic, that is, in his later terminology, as knowledge of the supra-sensible, a definition which moves away from Leibniz and the aforementioned Leibnizians. In the §59 of the *Critique of Judgment*, Kant explicitly rejects the use of the term *symbolic* adopted by the "modern logicians", like Daries and Baumgarten, who

---

[8] See Mancosu **1999**, p 8.
[9] See Klein **1968**.
[10] On Kant's philosophy as a whole I am strongly in debt with Torretti **1980**.
[11] Daries **1742**, § 99.
[12] Baumgarten **1739**, § 629.
[13] Wolff **1738**, § 287.
[14] Wolff, *Ibid.*, § 288.
[15] Wolff, *Ibid.*, § 289.
[16] Ak. II, 396 [Kant **1992**, p. 389]. Kant's works are quoted according to the edition of the Academy of Berlin, (quoted as Ak.); quotations of the first *Critique* follow the usual convention of designating the first and second editions with the letters A and B, respectively.

opposed *symbolic* and *intuitive* modes of representation. Kant claims that symbolic knowledge is a kind of intuitive knowledge and that intuitive knowledge must be opposed to discursive knowledge.

Kant states that all intuitions that fall under a priori philosophical concepts are schemes or symbols. According to Kant, there are two intuitive modes of representation, namely, the schematic and the symbolic modes. Both modes are exhibitions: the intuitive mode is accomplished either by a schematic mode, through *exhibition,* or by a symbolic mode, through mere *analogy*. The schemes are direct exhibitions of concepts of the understanding or categories (i.e., a priori philosophical concepts *with* objective reference); the symbols are indirect exhibitions of concepts of reason or ideas (i.e., a priori philosophical concepts *without* objective reference) by means of analogy. Without getting into the details concerning the concept of "indirect exhibition by analogy" as an emergency resource to our ideas of reason or concepts of the supra-sensible, it is important to highlight that such symbolic exhibitions for Kant are opposed to "mere characterisms". The latter are understood as visible signs or words (algebraic, and inclusively, mimic signs), which do not contain the intuition of the object and, therefore, are "mere expressions" of concepts.[17]

Mathematical knowledge is also schematic knowledge. One of the characterizations of a scheme in the *Critique* used in connection with mathematical concepts is a "representation of a universal proceeding of the imagination for providing a concept with its image".[18] Although Kant often refers to mathematical schemes, the official notion of the philosophy of mathematics of the *Critique* is "to construct a concept", defined as "to exhibit a priori the intuition corresponding to it",[19] a definition clearly compatible with the aforementioned characterization of a scheme. At first glance, the construction of a concept would yield an "instance" of it — to the extent that a pure image can be an instance.

These observations suggest that there is no place for symbolic knowledge according to Leibniz's sense. Nevertheless, the importance of signs and their manipulation in mathematical knowledge is not alien to Kant's mature thinking, for in the *Critique* he makes a distinction between *ostensive* construction and *symbolic* or *characteristic* construction: the first, proper to geometry, is a construction of the objects themselves; the second, proper to algebra, is a construction by means of signs. What about the philosophical understanding of symbolism in the pre-critical period? In contrast to the *Critique*, Kant's emphasis in the *Inquiry* is, as it will be shown, on the role of signs in *all* mathematical domains.[20]

---

[17] Cf. Ak. V, 254-260; see also *Anthropology from a pragmatic point of view*, §38, Ak.VII, 191. For a detailed account of symbolic knowledge in Kant's sense, cf. Lebrun **1993**, chap. VIII.
[18] A 140 / B 179 [Kant **1998**, p. 263].
[19] A 713 / B 741 [Kant **1998**, p. 630].
[20] Since the debate between Hintikka and Parsons leads one to rethink Kant's philosophy of mathematics and symbolic construction in the *Critique*, the literature on the subject has

2. Symbolic knowledge in the *Inquiry*

The *Inquiry* includes a discussion about the difference of the methods of philosophy and mathematics. In the *First reflection* there are four sections: the last is dedicated to a comparison between the objects of mathematics and those of philosophy; the first three are about their modes of definition, their non-analyzable concepts and indemonstrable propositions, and the use of signs in their demonstrations. One immediately perceives the similarity with the exposition of the same problem in *The Discipline of Pure Reason in Dogmatic Use,* a section of *The Transcendental Doctrine of Method*, which deals with definitions, axioms and demonstrations. As it is well known, Kant will conclude this section of the *Critique* by claiming that only mathematics provides definitions, possesses axioms and demonstrates. Kant's conclusions in the *Inquiry* are essentially the same, yet reached by different routes.

In the *Inquiry*, the object of mathematics is traditionally characterized as being quantity or magnitude.[21] Kant also appeals to the division of mathematics into two branches, that is, geometry and arithmetic. Kant also distinguishes between the arithmetic of numbers, in which we can determine the ratio (*Verhältnis*) of the magnitude or quantity to unity, and general (*allgemeine*) arithmetic of indeterminate magnitudes or quantities (*von den unbestimmten Grössen*). The characterization of arithmetic in terms of "determinate ratio of the magnitude to unity", i.e., in terms of the theory of commensurable magnitudes, implies that we should include not only natural numbers in its scope but, possibly, also fractions. The general arithmetic of indeterminate magnitudes is sometimes identified with algebra.[22] Kant claims:

---

occasionally been forced to consider the *Inquiry*. Hintikka distinguishes between a *preliminary theory* of mathematics in the *Inquiry*, which would survive in the *Transcendental Doctrine of Method*, and a *complete theory*, which would be found in the *Transcendental Aesthetic*. The main difference between the two theories is that, while Kant intended in the complete theory to show that all intuition is sensible, in the preliminary theory no connection between intuition and sensibility is assumed. In the preliminary theory, the definitory note of intuition would be individuality or singularity, that is, intuition would be everything that, in the human mind, represents or "stands for" an individual. In Hintikka **1969**, Leibniz's distinction between intuitive and symbolic knowledge is used to attribute the central note of individuality to Kant's notion of intuition. Besides Hintikka's impressive papers (Hintikka **1967, 1969, 1982, 1984**), the philosophy of mathematics of the *Inquiry* was incidentally considered by Parsons **1983**, Ferrarin **1995**, Friedman **1992**, Pierobon **2003**.

[21] Ak. II, 282.

[22] In support of his reading of algebra in the critical period, Friedman **1992**, p. 108 states that algebra is correlatively characterized in the *Inquiry* as the theory of incommensurable magnitudes, that is, the Eudoxian theory of proportions. Shabel **2003**, n. 56, pp. 165-166, argues against Friedman's reading that in the mathematical texts from Kant's time algebra "is typically included with trigonometry and calculus under the heading of "Analysis", while the theory of proportion is given within the (independent) discussion of arithmetic."

> In both kinds of arithmetic, there are posited first of all not things themselves but their signs, together with the special designations of their increase or decrease, their relations *etc*. Thereafter, one operates with these signs according to easy and certain rules, by means of substitution, combination, subtraction and many kinds of transformation, so that the things signified are themselves completely forgotten in the process, until eventually, when the conclusion is drawn, the meaning of the symbolic conclusion is deciphered.[23]

We find in this passage both the substitution of the things by signs and blind symbolic manipulation ("the things signified" are set aside to reappear in the conclusion with the reinterpretation of the signs). Thus, it is plausible to consider Kant's theses on mathematical knowledge in connection with the knowledge (or thinking) that Leibniz called *symbolic* or *blind*.

We can also provide further evidence in favor of our interpretation based on Kant's claims in *Attempt to introduce the concept of negative magnitudes into philosophy*, of 1763. Kant states there that the elucidations of the concept of negative magnitudes are strange and inconsistent. He goes on to say:

> This has not, however, resulted in any errors of application, for the particular rules governing its employment took the place of the definition and guaranteed its correct use.[24]

These rules (essentially, the rule of additive inverse) govern the signs "+" and "-". Kant's approach is broadly "structural": "Accordingly, in mathematics (*in der Grössenwissenschaft*) these two signs only serve to distinguish magnitudes which are opposed to each other, in other words, those magnitudes which, when combined, cancel each other either wholly or in part."[25]

In the *Inquiry*, Kant also refers to a general theory of magnitudes (*der allgemeinen Grössenlehre*) which would constitute the science of general arithmetic in the strict sense. Mathematics must be based on the fundamental principles of this general arithmetic. We can think that the treatment of the concept of negative magnitudes belongs to the general theory of magnitudes. The "theory of roots" is included in this "general cognition" and some

---

[23] Ak. II, 278 [Kant **1992**, p. 250].
[24] Ak. II, 170 [Kant **1992**, p.210].
[25] Ak. II, 173 [Kant **1992**, p.213].

fundamental concepts of space allow the application of this general arithmetic to geometry. We also find in the *Inquiry* an old expression related to algebra, i.e., the German translation of *calculus literalis* (*Buchstabenrechnung*). This "calculus with letters" is nothing but the old *logistice speciosa* which in the 17th century was usually opposed to the numerical calculus (*calculus numeralis, logistice numerosa*).

Are "general arithmetic of indeterminate magnitudes", "general theory of magnitudes" and "calculus with letters" synonymous to algebra for Kant? Many authors in the previous century made that identification. It seems to be safe to say that each of these terms presents aspects that were considered as part of the domain of algebra in the tradition leading up to Kant.[26] This is enough for us. In each case, we find the surrogating function of the signs and their manipulation without consideration of the designated, namely, what we called the 'computational function'.

Thus, we begin to grasp the similarity between Leibniz's and Kant's treatments regarding the arithmetical and algebraic symbolism. Yet it is important to notice that in the *Inquiry* geometric knowledge is also grounded in the surrogating function of the signs and in their manipulation, although this knowledge is not a completely blind one. In fact, geometrical figures are, for Kant, as well as for Leibniz, signs:

> Furthermore, in geometry the signs are similar to the things signified, so that the certainty of geometry is even greater, though the certainty of algebra (*Buchstabenrechnung*) is no less reliable.[27]

A figure can certainly be seen as *subsumed* under the corresponding concept, however the function of a figure *qua* sign is, according to Leibniz's terminology, to *express* a concept, and not to instantiate it. Kant does not only state that figures are signs, but also uses Leibniz's distinction between signs with similarity and signs without similarity or between signs with imitative similarity and with non-imitative similarity.[28] In particular, just as Leibniz, Kant considers that figures are signs with (imitative) similarity, in opposition to algebraic signs (and, presumably, to the usual arithmetical signs also) which are without (imitative) similarity. The following passage of Leibniz, extracted from *Dialogue* (1677) supports our interpretation:

---

[26] I am in debt in this point to P. Mancosu (personal e-mail correspondence). In Shabel **2003** we find an extensive study of the concept of algebra in the critical period in order to elucidate the concept of "symbolic construction"; however, unfortunately, she does not discuss the notion of algebra in the *Inquiry*. We agree with Shabel **2003**, p.164, n. 51: "Kant's pre-critical and critical views must be treated separately".
[27] Ak. II, 292 [Kant **1992**, p. 265].
[28] On *similarity* see Lebrun **1989**, pp. 46-50.

> B. Yet when we examine the figures of geometry, we sometimes establish truths merely by contemplating them accurately.
>
> A. True, but we must recognize that these figures must also be regarded as characters, for the circle described on paper is not a true circle and need not be; it is enough that we take it for a circle.
>
> B. Nevertheless, it has a certain similarity to the circle, and this is surely not arbitrary.
>
> A. Granted; therefore, figures are the most useful of characters. But what similarity do you think there is between ten and the character 10?
>
> B. There is some relation or order in the characters which is also in things, especially if the characters are well invented.[29]

In the *Dialogue* it is also stated that without words or other signs we cannot discover, know or demonstrate. Moreover, we can neither think "with distinction" nor ratiocinate. As a particular case, figures *should be considered* as characters, a fact which explains why "by strict meditation" we can, using them, obtain geometrical truths. Regarding the numeric or algebraic characters, there is no imitative similarity with the things denoted, for example, between the numeral 0 and "nothing", just as there is no similarity between the algebraic character *a* and the line which such character stands for. Nevertheless, Leibniz writes, "if characters can be used for ratiocination, there is in them a kind of complex mutual relation [*situs*] or order which fits the things; if not in the single words at least in their combination and inflection, although it is even better if found in the single words themselves".[30] And, according to Leibniz, the foundation of the truth, reached by means of characters, lies in such connections.

We showed that for Kant and for Leibniz mathematical knowledge involves the surrogating and computational functions of the signs in arithmetic as well as in algebra. In geometry the figures surrogate geometrical concepts and by their manipulation we also achieve symbolic knowledge. We must, in the sequel, examine the topic of the *ante oculos* certainty, which requires the consideration of the difference between mathematical signs and natural language signs, that is, words. There are two independent issues about the sensualization of thought that are conflated here.

Firstly, the *ante oculos* certainty derives from the visual inspection of the regulated use of mathematical characters. Such kind of certainty, proper to mathematics, derives from symbolic manipulation whose correctness can be

---

[29] A VI 4, 23; GP VII, 191-192 [Loemker **1969**, p. 184].
[30] A VI 4, 24; GP VII, 192 [Loemker **1969**, p. 184].

visually inspected. In other words, a calculus consists of the manipulation of characters according to certain rules and we can visually verify whether or not these rules have been correctly applied. Leibniz states:

> The only means of ordering our reasonings is to make them as perceptible as are the reasonings of the mathematicians, so that one can find their mistakes before one's very eyes; in this way, when there is a controversy among people, one could say only "let's count" without further ceremony, in order to determine who is right.[31]

Secondly, the *ante oculos* certainty also seems to derive from the mode of representation of concepts by means of mathematical language. Thus, sensualization also involves a dimension that connects it to the form of representation of concepts by mathematical signs. Leibniz named, as already mentioned, *ecthetic* this form of representation. In the symbolic language of mathematics, a formula shows the constituent concepts of a given concept, for example, "$(x + y) + z = x + (y + z)$" shows the constituent components of the concept "associativity of addition". The function of the *ecthetic* representation, according to Leibniz, is not at first *to designate*, as it is done by the words of natural language: it is a form of representation that, given its analytical nature, is adequate for the calculus, but is inadequate for articulated speech. Sensualization, from this perspective, consists of a sort of symbolic presentation of the components of a concept.

In the *Inquiry* we can find similar ideas. Kant contrasts mathematics, which considers *in concreto* its concepts *under signs*, with philosophy, which *in abstracto*, considers its concepts *by means of signs*:

> Mathematics, in its analyses, proofs and inferences examines the universal under signs *in concreto*; philosophy examines the universal by means of signs *in abstracto*.[32]

For Kant a mathematician can lay signs *in the place* of concepts and with them he can infer and demonstrate. The use of signs instead of concepts, as well as their manipulation which yields (symbolic) knowledge, also has for Kant this additional advantage:

> For since signs in mathematics are sensible means to cognition, it follows that one can know that no concept has been overlooked, and that each

---

[31] A VI 4, 964 [C 176]. Esquisabel's translation.
[32] Ak. II, 278 [Kant **1992**, p. 250].

> particular comparison has been drawn in accordance with easily observed rules *etc.* And these things can be known with the degree of assurance characteristic of seeing something with one's own eyes.[33]

Thus, mathematical signs are for Kant sensible means of knowledge. The sensualization of thought or ratiocination guarantees the correctness of our ratiocination in arithmetic, algebra and geometry and, consequently, *ante oculos* certainty.[34] This is the first issue that was mentioned before.

Philosophy lacks such kind of certainty which is derived from symbolic manipulation, for the philosopher's signs are precisely the words of natural language: this is the reason why he must consider concepts *in abstracto*, *by means of* signs, and not *in concreto*, *under* signs, as the mathematician may do. In order to explain the difference between the signs in philosophy and mathematics, Kant states in the *Inquiry*:

> The signs employed in philosophical reflection are never anything other than words. And words can neither show in their composition the constituent concepts of which the whole idea, indicated by the word, consists; nor are they capable of indicating in their combinations the relation of the philosophical thoughts to each other.[35]

The terms, in which the comparison between the signs used by philosophers and the ones used by mathematicians is made, are significant. Kant repeats the objections formulated against natural language by the theoreticians of the *lingua universalis* in the 17th century, as well as by

---

[33] Ak. II, 291 [Kant **1992**, p. 265].

[34] Parsons observes that the thesis of the *Inquiry*, namely, that in mathematics the operation with signs according to rules, without paying attention to what they mean, is enough to assure its certainty, is incompatible with the position of the *Critique*. We also agree with Parsons that the mathematical certainty in the *Inquiry* is related to the fact that signs are sensible (Parsons **1983**, p. 138). In fact, the surrogating function, the acquired knowledge through symbolic manipulation, and the *ante oculos* certainty of such knowledge are all Leibnizian topics. When criticizing (as dispensable) Hintikka's interpretation of the *Inquiry*, based on the three last aforementioned passages, Parsons states that such passages betray a connection in Kant's mind between sensibility and the intuitive character of mathematics before the development of his theory of space and time of the *Transcendental Aesthetic*. Our reading certainly does justice to the aspects highlighted by Parsons. However, it also allows us to dispense with the vague connection proposed by him between sensibility and intuitivity of mathematics. Pierobon states that, in the *Inquiry*, the mode of evidence of geometry lies in a "phénoménologie du voir"; in which we have, in front of our eyes, the geometrical things themselves (cf. Pierobon **2003**, p. 43). There are no such "things themselves", there is sensualization of concepts by means of signs with (imitative) similarity.

[35] Ak. II, 278-279 [Kant **1992**, p. 251].

Leibniz, claiming that the words of natural language do not represent concepts directly. A philosophical word such as "time", Kant states, does not show the concepts that make up the very concept of time, in contrast with what the mathematical signs do with their corresponding concepts. The word "associativity" does not do that either, while the formula $(x+y)+z=x+(y+z)$ shows the constitutive concepts of associativity itself. Thus, we go back to the aforementioned second issue of sensualization of thought, that is, that the form of representation of the mathematical formulae is *ecthetic*, at least in its way of expressing a given designated.

We hold that this "knowledge under signs" is (or is in the tradition of) Leibnizian symbolic knowledge. Although we do not have in Kant any kind of "intuition of ideas", and in this sense no intuitive knowledge, we have in its place some kind of access to concepts by means of reflection. We can replace this "consideration of the universal *in abstracto*" by signs and manipulate them to reach knowledge with *ante oculos* certainty. What kind of symbolic knowledge is this? We showed that we have symbolic knowledge in the sense of a succedaneum of the direct consideration of concepts in arithmetic and elementary geometry. Is there any place for symbolic knowledge in the full sense of formal knowledge? Well, we can only say that the extremely liberal theory of mathematical concept formation, the central role performed by signs in the *Inquiry* and the idea of a general cognition associated with a general theory of magnitudes strongly suggest this possibility.[36] We do not find any indications of symbolic knowledge as an instrumental extension of the intuitive knowledge in Kant.[37]

3. On philosophical and mathematical methods

In a letter to Burnet, Leibniz also uses the expression "*ecthetic* demonstration" to refer to demonstrations that use characters that represent in an *ecthetic* manner, distinguishing them from "conceptual demonstrations", which use natural language.[38] The first type of demonstration is realized by means of transposition and substitution (manipulation) of the characters of the *ecthetic* expression, while the second is realized by the consideration of the concepts fixed by its definition. If we recall that figures are also characters (or should be considered as such) with (imitative) similarity, we then realize that we could subsume a geometrical demonstration (at least partially) as well as an algebraic or arithmetical one under the concept of "*ecthetic* demonstration".

Can one assume from reading the last three passages that Kant reproduces Leibniz's distinction between *ecthetic* and conceptual

---

[36] And the idea of a general geometry also suggests this: Ak I, 24. See Torretti **1980**, pp. 93-97.
[37] Section 2 presents a helpful improved version of Lassalle Casanave **2007**.
[38] GP III, 258.

demonstrations? Kant would certainly admit that in mathematics we have the two classes of demonstrations. The philosophical arguments are conceptual only under a given perspective: they are developed *by means of words*, yet they cannot omit the consideration of the concepts which those words designate, for the words do not represent the partial constituent concepts of the "whole idea" that they designate, nor the combination of words represent the relationship between "philosophical thoughts". But Kant, in contrast to Leibniz, was not postulating a *more geometrico* regulation of natural language through definitions.

In fact, Kant's defense of the autonomy of the philosophical method in the *Inquiry* rejects the possibility of conceiving philosophical definitions along the lines of Euclidean definitions. Kant states that, while the content of philosophical concepts is *given,* the content of mathematical concepts is *not given*, but rather introduced by (synthetic) definition. A mathematical definition arbitrarily composes notes and such composition is subjected to the principle of non-contradiction. The definition delimits in an exhaustive and complete way the concept in question and there is no mathematical concept previous to its definition. On the contrary, the (analytic) definition of a philosophical concept would be the result of the analysis of the pre-analytically given content of the concept: "In philosophy, the concept of a thing is always given, albeit confusedly or in insufficiently determinate fashion."[39]

The analysis is the philosophical task of conceptual clarification and it is always tentative due to the nature of the concepts involved; the nature of philosophical concepts makes it impossible to start from definitions that intend to completely draw out the content of philosophical concepts by decomposition. The definition of a philosophical concept in the rather doubtful case that it could be achieved would be the conclusion of the philosophical task instead of its methodical starting point. For similar reasons, there are no axioms in philosophy. We have, of course, evident and immediate propositions about philosophical concepts, which are neither exhaustive nor complete as mathematical axioms would be. Therefore, the philosophical method cannot start from definitions and axioms, in the style illustrated by Spinoza's famous *Ethica* or by today's less famous works of Wolff and the Wolffian school. Thus, according to Kant, there are no conceptual demonstrations in Leibniz's sense in philosophy.

It is obvious that there are no *ecthetic* demonstrations in philosophy also, as seen by the difference between mathematical language and natural language. Nevertheless, the same considerations regarding the nature of philosophical concepts allow us to see that Kant also rejects the project of a *more algebrico* philosophy. The Leibnizian semiotic and epistemology culminated in a natural manner in the idea of a *lingua universalis* that would simultaneously be a *calculus ratiocinator,* that is, an *ars characteristica*

---

[39] Ak. II, 276 [Kant **1992**, p. 248].

universalis. Leibniz did not want only a language that allowed a universal communication, but also a language that permitted calculation. In light of the difficulties of realizing the general project, he also considered partial realizations of it.

The temptation of extending algebraic formalism as a tool to every area of knowledge, especially the philosophical one, gives rise to exactly this project: a language with a universal scope, free from ambiguity, that exempts us from the consideration of the corresponding ideas, and whose well governed manipulation allows us to reach truths. One could compare algebraic formalism to natural language. This is restricted to its corresponding community, inevitably subjected to ambiguity, whose signs (words) can neither be used without ignoring their meaning nor do they admit a calculus. Who could resist the alluring spell of a philosophically perfect language? Kant could.

In *A new elucidation of the first principles of metaphysical cognition*, dated 1755, Kant is skeptical about the Leibnizian project of an *ars characteristica*.[40] In the *Inquiry*, the peculiarity of philosophical concepts we have referred to reminds us the problem of the "simplest concepts", i.e., of the supreme genus needed for an *ars characteristica universalis* that occupied Wilkins and Leibniz. This philosophical variant of the *Problem of the Encyclopedia* excludes the possibility that philosophy might use algebraic methods. Hence, there cannot be *ecthetic* demonstrations in philosophy.[41]

In the *Critique*, Kant returns to the distinction between given and not-given (content of) concepts adopting a different approach. Philosophical concepts are concepts whose content are given and can be subjected to analysis by the decomposition of their notes. Mathematical concepts are not-given; rather they are *constructed*. As in the *Inquiry*, there is no mathematical concept before its definition, although mathematical definition now is an arbitrary synthesis by the construction of concepts *in intuition*. Just like in the *Inquiry*, the philosopher, according to the *Critique*, cannot provide

---

[40] See Ak. I, 389-390.

[41] In Ferrarin **1995**, p. 133, we read that the distinctive evidence that makes mathematics an exact science only depends on univocity, immediate verifiability and visibility of their signs opposing the indetermination of the words that the metaphysicist must use, which cannot analyze the philosophical concepts in their elementary constituents. The notes that Ferrarin attributes to mathematical signs confirm our proposal, although we believe that the "philosophical versus mathematical language" question and its entailment with the methodological distinction between philosophy and mathematics is better understood under our interpretation. We coincide also with Ferrarin when he states that, in the *Inquiry*, there is a lack of the conception of pure intuition in which we can construct mathematical objects and, then, the meaning of the term "synthesis" in the *Inquiry* is different from the *Critique*. For this, we dissent from him on the possibility of finding in the arbitrary character of signs and in the synthetic origin of mathematical concepts in the *Inquiry* the germ of the notion of "constructing a concept in intuition".

definitions; however, the difference between mathematics and philosophy is now characterized as follows:

> Philosophical cognition thus considers the particular only in the universal, but mathematical cognition considers the universal in the particular, indeed even in the individual, yet nonetheless a priori and by means of reason, so that just as this individual is determined under certain general conditions of construction, the object of the concept, to which this individual corresponds only as its schema, must likewise be thought as universally determined.[42]

If the task of philosophy in the *Inquiry* was defined as the clarification of concepts, in the *Critique* Kant affirms that the task of philosophy is not that of clarifying concepts, but rather that of validating our knowledge. Such enlargement demands as a necessary condition that rational concepts (metaphysical or mathematical) be linked to intuition: philosophical schemes or mathematical constructions.

The refusal to regulate natural language *more geometrico* with definitions is maintained in the *Critique*, although from a different perspective, for a definition does not fulfill the task of regulating the terms of natural language as it does in the *Inquiry*, but rather proves the objective reality of the defined concept.[43] As in the *Inquiry*, in the *Critique*, the philosopher does not employ axioms either, where the latter are understood as immediate and evident principles in intuition. There are axioms only in mathematics (in geometry, to be exact) and the philosophical principles must also be proved. Finally, just like in the *Inquiry*, in the *Critique*, Kant claims that philosophical proofs and mathematical demonstrations are not alike:

> Philosophical cognition, on the contrary, must do without this advantage, since it must always consider the universal *in abstracto* (through concepts), while mathematics can assess the universal *in concreto* (in the individual intuition) and yet through pure *a priori* intuition, where every false step becomes visible. Since they can only be conducted by means of mere words (the

---

[42] A 714 / B742 [Kant **1998**, p. 631].

[43] In the *Inquiry*, the fact that the mathematical method is settled on replacing concepts by signs (figures, in particular) does not seem enough to historically ground Hintikka's hypothesis about the meaning of the term "intuition" in Kant's mature philosophy: it actually seems to testify the opposite. The contrast with the *Inquiry* could not be greater, for in the *Critique*, a figure is the result of constructing a concept, it is not a sign.

> object in thought), I would therefore prefer to call the former **acroamatic** (discursive) proofs rather than **demonstration**, which, as the expression already indicates, proceeds through the intuition of the object.[44]

The methodological implications of the difference between the mathematicians' language and the philosophers' language (natural language) were central to the *Inquiry*. In the *Critique*, this difference still persists, although the emphasis in the distinction between philosophy and mathematics is grounded on the way in which they link intuitions to their respective concepts. It is true that in a letter to Beck, dated September 1791, Kant says that since we have the complete table of categories and ideas of reason, mathematics can offer philosophy new methods of representation, something like the *ars characteristica combinatoria*. But Kant holds that a *characteristica philosophica* can only elucidate, but not enlarge, our metaphysical knowledge.[45]

In short: in the *Inquiry*, mathematical knowledge is under signs and philosophical knowledge is by means of signs; in the *Critique*, mathematical knowledge is by (ostensive or symbolic) construction of concepts and philosophical knowledge is by concepts.

4. Knowledge by symbolic construction in the *Critique*

Mathematical concepts are linked to intuition by construction. In the case of geometry, Kant abandons the Leibnizian thesis of the *Inquiry* in which the figures are signs or characters that stand for concepts; the figures will be conceived as intuitions corresponding to concepts (ostensive construction). The figures are *exhibitions* of the concepts, instead of expressions of the concepts. Thus, in *On a Discovery According to which Any New Critique of Pure Reason Has Been Made Superfluous by an Earlier One* (henceforth *On a Discovery*), for example, while commenting on construction of the concept of cone as a preliminary step to the construction of the parabola, Kant writes:

> Appollonius first constructs the concept of a cone, i.e., he exhibits it a priori in intuition (this is the first operation by means of which the geometer presents in advance the objective reality of his concepts).[46]

---

[44] A 734 / B 762 – A 735 / B 763 [Kant **1998**, p. 632].
[45] See Ak. XI, 290.
[46] Ak. VIII, 191 [Allison **1973**, p. 110].

Kant also abandons in the *Critique* the preeminence of the notational apparatus in the grounding of the arithmetic of natural numbers in favor of the intuitions corresponding to arithmetical concepts. The arithmetical construction could be linked to the activity of *enumeration*. Thus, the ostensive construction of numerical concepts is the exhibition of strokes or dot sequences, and the ostensive construction of the sum, for example, consists of overlapping those sequences and afterwards in enumerating them to obtain the result, the usual calculus with arithmetical signs possibly being conceived as a secondary device.[47]

What about the analytical methods of "modern geometers" (algebraists) of introducing geometrical entities by signs? In *On a Discovery* Kant, for instance, writes:

> One could rather address to the modern geometers a reproach of the following nature: not that they derive the properties of a curved line from its definition without first being assured of the possibility of its object (for they are fully conscious of this together with the pure, merely schematic construction, and they also bring in mechanical construction afterwards if it is necessary), but that they arbitrarily think for themselves such a line (e.g., the parabola through the formula $ax = y^2$), and do not, according to the example of ancient geometers, first bring it forth as given in the conic section.[48]

Therefore, the algebraic procedure must be linked to intuition: the symbolic apparatus of algebra is conceived as a symbolic construction by means of signs. The Leibnizian tradition of symbolic knowledge pointed out in the previous sections reappears in the notion of symbolic construction. Kant claims that this kind of construction is specifically related to algebra:

> But mathematics does not merely construct magnitudes (*quanta*), as in geometry, but also mere magnitude (*quantitatem*), as in algebra (*Buchtabenrechnung*), where it entirely abstracts from the constitution of the object that is to be thought in accordance with such a concept of magnitude. In this case it chooses a certain

---

[47] For details of the distinction between enumerating and calculating, see Young **1982**, where we find an interesting attempt at extending symbolic construction to arithmetical concepts. We examine Young's attempt in Lassalle Casanave **2006**.
[48] Ak. VIII, 192 [Allison **1973**, p. 111].

> notation for all construction of magnitudes in general (numbers), as well as addition, subtraction, extraction of roots, etc., and, after it has also designated the general concept of quantities in accordance with their different relations, it then exhibits all the procedures through which magnitude is generated and altered in accordance with certain rules in intuition; where one magnitude is to be divided by another, it places their symbols together in accordance with the form of notation for division, and thereby achieves by a symbolic construction equally well what geometry does by an ostensive or geometrical construction (of the objects themselves), which discursive cognition could never achieve by means of mere concepts.[49]

In this passage, it becomes explicit that the surrogating function is assumed in such type of construction and that the governed manipulation of signs, namely, the computational function of the symbolism, produces mathematical knowledge. By means of the manipulation of algebraic signs we obtain a kind of knowledge which we can call *knowledge by symbolic construction*, in order to differentiate Kant's mature conception from Leibniz's conception of symbolic knowledge as formal knowledge. In the other passage on symbolic construction concerning the distinction between philosophical and mathematical proofs discussed at the end of the previous section, Kant states that this kind of knowledge exhibits *ante oculos* certainty:

> Even the way algebraists (*Verfahren der Algebra*) proceed with their equations, from which by means of reduction they bring forth the truth together with the proof, is not a geometrical construction, but is still a characteristic construction, in which one displays by signs in intuition the concepts, especially of relations of quantities, and, without even regarding the heuristic, secures all inferences against mistakes by placing each of them before one's eyes.[50]

In this second passage, we also find, in addition to the *ante oculos* certainty, the heuristic import of an adequate symbolism: such function

---

[49] A717 / B 745 [Kant **1998**, p. 632].
[50] A734 / B762 [Kant **1998**, p. 641].

could be included in the scope of the psychotechnic function of symbolic knowledge. Nevertheless, Kant adds a further condition in these passages, namely, that the symbolic exhibition of the generation and alteration of magnitudes must run parallel with the rules in intuition for such generation and alteration. The symbolic construction in algebra is an indirect exhibition *by rules of symbolic manipulation* of the corresponding quantities abstracting from their qualities (then, mere quantity or magnitude).[51] This symbolic procedure, which is governed by rules, runs parallel to ostensive (instantial) constructions. Thus, knowledge by symbolic construction is symbolic knowledge as a succedaneum of ostensive knowledge.

Elucidation of these matters requires clearing up what we should understand by algebra in the *Critique*. The classical objection to characteristic or symbolic construction is that Kant seems to abandon the instantial sense of "to construct a concept" and that the newly sense introduced does not have any relation to the original conception of construction.[52] The "prevailing view" on symbolic construction presupposes that symbolic construction is a manipulation of the algebraic symbolism *without ostensive counterpart*.[53] As a starting point, we do not consider algebra as a theory on its own right; we shall speak of algebraic method for the resolution of arithmetical and geometrical problems instead.[54]

For instance, considering algebra as a method of solving geometrical problems in a Cartesian way, we replace the unknown and the known magnitudes of the given problem by signs. This step, called *naming,* is the first of the three steps of Descartes' procedure.[55] The second step is *equating*: it consists in expressing the unknown magnitude(s) in terms of the known ones, which is reached by governed manipulation of signs. Thus, we have the computational function and the *ante oculos* certainty. The concepts

---

[51] In a letter to Reinhold, of 1789, Kant writes: "The mathematician cannot make the least claim in regard to any object whatsoever without exhibiting it in intuition (or, if we are dealing merely with quantities without qualities, as in algebra (*wie in der Algebra*), exhibiting the quantitative relationships thought under the chosen symbols)." Ak. XI, 42 [*Apud* Allison **1973**, p. 167].

[52] In Broad **1978**, pp. 69-70, we find these classical objections. Broad concludes that Kant has nothing to say about algebra and about the algebraic ratiocination.

[53] See the complete account on this view in Shabel **2003**, pp. 117-123. To avoid Broad's conclusion about symbolic construction, Hintikka considers algebra as a theory whose domain consists of numbers, while Friedman **1992** considers it as the theory of proportions of Eudoxos. Brittan **1992** dreams of more things than Kant's philosophy knows: he talks about algebra as consisting of sets on which certain iterable operations are defined.

[54] In her study on the historical roots of the Kantian concept of algebra, Shabel **2003** shows that no further arguments are needed to defend this starting point. Our analysis of symbolic construction essentially agrees in this point with that of Shabel **2003**, yet we arrive at it from the perspective of the aforementioned functions associated with symbolic knowledge. We do not intend here to reproduce her sophisticated argumentation, but we think that a very simplified presentation is enough to defend our interpretation regarding the philosophical roots of symbolic construction.

[55] For details to these steps, see Mancosu **1998**, pp. 67-68.

which are involved in the equations are addition, subtraction, root extraction, etc., mentioned in A717 / B745. A notation for such concepts is chosen and exhibits the procedure by which a magnitude is transformed or generated *in accordance with certain rules in intuition* by means of signs. Finally, the third step is *constructing* the equation, that is, to find geometrically its roots. Thus, we can easily understand Kant's claim in A734 / B762 that the algebraic method yields the truth also with the proof by means of symbolic construction.[56] We can extend these steps to the solution of arithmetical problems. In this case, in the final step, we have enumeration (with strokes or points) or calculation (with numerical signs) instead of geometrical construction. Thus, the algebraic formula both in geometry and arithmetic exhibits symbolically the corresponding intuition, namely, it has an *ecthetic* function, at least *in principle*.

In fact, to achieve the solution of a problem it is necessary to give a construction in geometry or to enumerate (or to calculate) in arithmetic the symbolically expressed magnitude, for algebraic manipulation does not always result in a possible geometrical construction or an arithmetical calculus or an enumeration. This point is illustrated in a letter to Rehberg, dated 1790, where the following problem is considered: to find two equal factors whose product is equal to **a**, that is, to find the proportional mean between 1 and **a**, that is, $1 : x = x : \mathbf{a}$. At once, algebraically, $\mathbf{a} = x^2$, and then $x = \sqrt{\mathbf{a}}$. In particular, $\sqrt{2}$ is the proportional mean between 1 and 2. In geometry, the proportional mean between a line segment of length 2 and a unit segment can be constructed following, for example, the Cartesian procedure of root construction in *La Géométrie*. That shows that $\sqrt{2}$ is a non-empty concept, i.e., it has objective reference. The problem is why a number representing such a quantity cannot be found.

Rehberg's question was, as interpreted by Kant, why we are able to think $\sqrt{2}$ in numbers and why the Understanding is not able to produce it, having to fall back into an increasing sequence of approximations. Kant says that the reason has to do with time, that is, with the successive progression as the form of every calculation and of every numerical quantity. Yet, as represented in algebra, the mere square root concept of a positive quantity, that is, $\sqrt{\mathbf{a}}$, does not require any temporal synthesis, which leaves arithmetic in a different situation:

---

[56] In Lachterman **1989**, p. 11, we read: "I merely note here that Kant takes his understanding of the technique of construction from *algebra* (and not, therefore, from "traditional" geometry or arithmetic). Kant's phrase "construction of a concept" is derived from the expression "construction of an [algebraic] equation", which he employs on occasion. This latter expression, taken from Christian Wolff, refers not to putting together the equation but to the interpretation of the terms of equation in ways that lead to the actual exhibition of a particular geometrical formation satisfying the general equation." To what extent Kant is conscious of the real import of the Cartesian procedure is not clear to us. See, for example, the vindication of the ancient geometers in *On a Discovery* quoted above.

> But as soon as, instead of *a*, the number for which *a* stands is given, so that the square root is not simply to be *named* (as in algebra (*wie in der Algebra*)) but calculated (as in arithmetic), the condition of all producing of numbers, viz., time, becomes the inescapable foundations of this process.[57]

We can also say that if, instead of *a,* the segment for which *a* stands is given, so that the square root is not simply to be *named* (as in algebra) but constructed (as in geometry), space, i.e. the condition of the production of lines, becomes the inescapable foundation of this process.

Ostensive constructions underlie the symbolic construction proper to the algebraic method, depending on the kind of problem whose solution we seek. When the application of the method occurs in arithmetic, the ostensive counterpart is enumeration (or calculus); when it occurs in geometry, it is related to geometrical construction. In the *Critique*, the surrogating function of the signs always requires an intuitive counterpart and the verification that the algebraic manipulation did not lead us to contradictory concepts or beyond "the possible experience"; this is achieved by means of an enumeration (or calculus) or by a geometrical construction.[58] In this way algebra, understood as a method of solving arithmetical and geometrical problems, can be founded on symbolic construction. We have not identified here intuitive knowledge simply as knowledge by ostensive construction. Thus, knowledge by symbolic construction and knowledge by ostensive construction are cases of (a kind of) intuitive schematic knowledge. The distinction is only a question of emphasis.[59]

---

[57] Ak. XI, 209 [Zweig **1967**, p. 16].

[58] The square root concept of a negative magnitude is self-contradictory, namely, it is an impossible quantity (Zweig **1967**, p.167). Thus, of course, $\sqrt{-a}$ does not surrogate. There is no attempt to introduce imaginary magnitudes in terms of fictitious ratios.

[59] Although Kant has never explicitly attributed to arithmetic the sort of characteristic or symbolic construction, the secondary literature has hypothetically assumed such possibility. An interpretation of Kant's philophy of arithmetic in terms of symbolic construction should then take into account three factors: a) the ostensive ground of arithmetic; b) the relevance of the notation, c) the connection between the symbolic manipulation and the synthetic character of arithmetic. A possible strategy would be to recognize that, in arithmetic, both types of construction are involved, ostensive and symbolic; see Young **1982**. In this case, of course, we would also have knowledge by symbolic construction as succedaneum of intuitive knowledge. The very indirect support for an interpretation of symbolic construction by analogy to numerical calculation, criticized by Shabel **2003**, is only a consequence of the computational function associated with symbolic knowledge. We do not offer any support to extend symbolic construction to logic as in Broad **1978** or Young **1982**.

5. Concluding remarks

As we have seen in the *Inquiry*, Kant conceives mathematical knowledge as essentially symbolic knowledge. In this and other works of the period, symbolic manipulation achieves that autonomy which is the condition of possibility for talking of symbolic knowledge as knowledge of structures or forms and not only as a succedaneum or as an instrumental extension of intuitive knowledge. If mathematics shares the fate of metaphysics then it is not surprising that Kant could admit in that period some knowledge of the supra-sensible. Nor should one be surprised that the restriction of metaphysical knowledge to the realm of the sensible was associated with a conception of mathematical knowledge as intuitive knowledge, just as it is found in the *Critique*.

Nevertheless, as we also see, a variant of Leibniz's symbolic knowledge survives the critical solution for the grounding of algebra. It is necessary to differentiate the *ecthesis* in geometry (and its corresponding form in arithmetic) from the *ecthesis* in algebra: the first is understood *sub specie* of intuition in the Kantian technical sense; the second, subordinated to the previous, is understood *sub specie* of sign. The *knowledge by symbolic construction* is symbolic knowledge as a succedaneum of ostensive knowledge. Thus, Kant can speak of the exhibition of the intuition corresponding to a concept *in both cases*, ostensive and symbolic. The consequence of the restrictions formulated in the *Critique* is meant, of course, to set limits to the autonomy of algebraic symbolism.

References

Allison, H. 1973. *The Kant-Eberhard Controversy*. Baltimore: Johns Hopkins University Press. Quoted as Allison **1973**.

Baumgarten, A. G. 1739 *Metaphysica*, Halle.

Belaval, I. 1960. *Leibniz Critique de Descartes*. Paris: Gallimard.

Brittan, G. 1992. "Algebra and Intuition". In C. POSY (ed.), *Kant's Philosophy of Mathematics: Modern Essays*. Dordrecht: Kluwer Academic Publishers, pp. 315-339.

Broad, C. D. 1978. *Kant. An introduction*. Cambridge: Cambridge University Press.

Daries. 1742. *Introductio in Artem inveniendi seu logicam theoretico-practicam, qua analytica atque dialectica in usum et jussu*. Jena.

Dascal. M. 1987. *Language, Signs and Thoughts. A Collection of Essays.* Amsterdam-Philadelphia: John Benjamín P. Co.

Esquisabel, O. M. 1999. *Del lenguaje racional a la ciencia de las fórmulas.* Tesis de Doctorado, Universidad Nacional de La Plata.

Ferrarin, A. 1995. "Construction and Mathematical Schematism. Kant on the Exhibition of a Concept in Intuition", *Kant-Studien* 86: 131-174.

Friedman, M. 1992. *Kant and the Exact Sciences.* Cambridge, MA: Harvard University Press.

Hintikka, J. 1967. "Kant on the mathematical method". In C. POSY (ed.), *Kant's Philosophy of Mathematics: Modern Essays.* Dordrecht: Kluwer Academic Publishers, pp. 21-42.

------------------ 1969. "On Kant's notion of intuition (*Anschauung*)". In T. PENELHUM and J. MAC INTOSH (eds.), *The First Critique: Reflections on Kant's "Critique of Pure Reason".* Belmont (CA): Wadsworth.

------------------ 1982. "Kant's Theory of Mathematics Revisited". In J. N. MOHANTY and R. W. SHELDAN (eds.), *Essays on Kant's Critique of Pure Reason.* Oklahoma: University of Oklahoma Press.

------------------ 1984. "Kant's Transcendental Method and his theory of mathematics". In C. POSY (ed.), *Kant's Philosophy of Mathematics: Modern Essays.* Dordrecht: Kluwer Academic Publishers, pp. 341-359.

Kant, I. 1968. *Kant's gesammelte Schriften, herausgegeben von der Preussischen Akademie der Wissenschaften.* Berlin 1902 ff., reimpr. Walter de Gruyter.

------------ 1969. *Kant: Philosophical Correspondence 1759-99*, edited by A. Zweig. Chicago: University of Chicago Press. Quoted as Zweig **1967**.

------------ 1992. *Theoretical philosophy, 1755-1770* Cambridge: Cambridge University Press. Quoted as Kant **1992**.

------------ 1998. *Critique of Pure Reason.* Cambridge: Cambridge University Press. Quoted as Kant **1998**.

Klein, J. 1968. *Greek Mathematical Thought and the Origin of Algebra.* New York: Dover Publications, Inc.

Lachterman, D. R. 1989. *The Ethics of Geometry. A Genealogy of Modernity*. New York and London: Routledge.

Lassalle Casanave, A. 2007. "Conhecimento simbólico na *Investigação* de 1764", *Analytica* 11 (1): 53-71.

------------ 2006. "Conocimiento por construcción simbólica" in M. DOFFI (comp.), *Lógica, epistemología y filosofía del lenguaje*. Buenos Aires: EUDEBA.

Lebrun, G. 1993. *Kant e o fim da metafísica*. São Paulo: Martins Fontes.

------------ 1989. "A noção de "Semelhança" de Descartes a Leibniz". In M. DASCAL (org.), *Conhecimento, Linguagem, Ideologia*. São Paulo: Perspectiva.

Leibniz, Gottfreid Wilhelm. 1903. *Opuscules et fragments inédits*, ed. by Louis Couturat. Paris (repr. by Georg Olms Verlag, Hildesheim/New York. 1988).

Leibniz, Gottfried Wilhelm Leibniz. 1969. *Philosophical Papers and Letters*, ed. by Leroy E. Loemker. Dordrecht/Boston/London, D. Reidel Publishing Company. Quoted as Loemker **1969**.

Leibniz, Gottfried Wilhelm. 1843-63. *Mathematische Schriften*, vols. 1-7, edited by C. I. Gerhardt. Berlin und Halle (repr. by Georg Olms Verlag, Hildesheim/New York. 1971).

Leibniz, Gottfried Wilhelm. 1875-1890. *Philosophische Schriften*, vols. 1-7, edited by C. I. Gerhardt. Berlin (repr. by Georg Olms Verlag, Hildesheim/New York. 1978)

Leibniz, Gottfried Wilhelm. 1923. *Sämtliche Schriften und Briefe*, edited by the German Academy of Sciences in Berlin, since 1923.

Mancosu, P. 1999. *Philosophy of Mathematics & Mathematical Practice in the Seventeenth Century*. New York: Oxford University Press.

Paton, H. J. 1961. *Kant's Metaphysic of Experience. A Commentary on the First Half of the Kritik der reinen Vernunft*. London: George Allen & Unwin Ltda.

Parsons, Ch. 1983. "Kant's Philosophy of Arithmetic", in C. POSY (ed.) (1992), *Kant's Philosophy of Mathematics: Modern Essays*. Dordrecht: Kluwer Academic Publishers, pp. 43-79.

Pierobon, F. 2003. *Kant et les mathématiques*. Paris: Vrin.

Shabel, L. 1998. "Kant on the 'Symbolic Construction' of Mathematical Concepts", *Stud. Hist. Phil. Sci.* 29(4): 589-621.

------------ 2003. *Mathematics in Kant's critical philosophy: reflections on mathematical practice*. London and New York: Routledge.

Torretti, R. 1980. *Manuel Kant. Estudio sobre los fundamentos de la filosofía crítica.* Buenos Aires: Editorial Charcas.

Wolff, Chr. 1738. *Psychologia Empirica*. Frankfurt und Leipzig (reimp. Olms 1968).

Young, J. M. 1982. "Kant on the Construction of Arithmetical Concepts", *Kant-Studien* 73: 17-46.

3

Between Calculus and Semantic Analysis

Symbolic Knowledge in the Origins of Mathematical Logic[*]

JAVIER LEGRIS

The aim of this chapter is to apply the notion of symbolic knowledge, conceived by G. W. Leibniz, to the understanding of some problems in the origins of mathematical (symbolic) logic in the 19th Century. In this sense, it can be regarded as a collection of notes for the study of the origins of mathematical logic with the notion of symbolic knowledge as *Leitfaden*. With its introduction I also hope to contribute to the current discussion in historiography of mathematical logic, where several distinctions, like the distinction between calculus and universal language, played an important role.

I will not discuss the specific contributions to symbolic logic made by the different authors mentioned in the paper. Therefore, their respective systems will not be introduced and their properties will not be investigated. Instead, I will trace the notion of symbolic knowledge that can be found implicitly in the work of three big pioneers of mathematical logic: George Boole, Ernst Schröder and Gottlob Frege. It should be noticed that even in the case of these leading figures in the origins of symbolic logic who explicitly

---

[*] Versions of different parts of this paper were presented at the Colóquios Conesul de Filosofia das Ciências Formais, Santa Maria, Brazil. I have greatly benefited from lively discussions during the last years with Jairo Da Silva, Oscar M. Esquisabel and Abel Lassalle Casanave Paolo Mancosu and Volker Peckhaus have been kind enough to read earlier drafts and their comments helped me to improve my exposition. I am also grateful to Ignacio Angelleli and Danielle Macbeth for helpful and valuable comments of an earlier draft of this paper. This work is part of the research project "Formal Calculus and Symbolic Knowledge in the History of Modern Logic", supported by the Consejo Nacional de Investigaciones Científicas y Técnicas (CONICET, Argentina). It was also partially supported by the Deutscher Akademischer Austausch Dienst (DAAD, Germany) and the Fundación Antorchas (Argentina).

borrowed ideas from Leibniz, the notion of symbolic knowledge is hardly mentioned. The case of Frege reveals itself as specially challenging because of Frege's withdrawal from this notion. It will be argued that his ideas on concept formation based on the analysis of judgeable contents are clearly distinguished from the methodology of symbolic knowledge.

In few words, symbolic knowledge can be roughly described as knowledge obtained by means of a formal calculus, understood as a procedure for the production of figures on the basis of basic figures according to a certain prescription, the basic rules. Every figure is composed from a stock of basic signs or basic figures. The figures obtain from composition of signs according to a set of rules in a *very* general sense. There is no presupposition about the nature of these figures or what they represent.[1] This conception is an essential part of the tradition of symbolic knowledge.

Leibniz contrasted symbolic knowledge with intuition or intuitive knowledge. This is an important feature of symbolic knowledge that I would like to emphasize here. This kind of knowledge emerges in fact when the complexity of the notions to be grasped is too high to have an intuition of them. This feature of symbolic knowledge will also be found in mathematical logicians of the 19th Century.

A problem underlying the whole discussion about symbolic knowledge, as knowledge by formal calculus, is the tension between the two notions of *computation* and *structure* not only in the history of logic but also in the origins of modern mathematics. There is a tension between two tendencies in constructing symbolic languages: on the one side, symbolic languages are constructed in order to make computations more efficient, on the other side, symbolic languages have the function of showing an underlying formal structure. Both tendencies are features of symbolic knowledge.

Symbolic logic emerged – under very complex conditions - from the convergence of different ideas and tendencies that involved both mathematics and philosophy. As Volker Peckhaus wrote, the 19th Century symbolic logic was "between mathematics and philosophy" (see Peckhaus 1999), that is, it received the influence of different problems in the two disciplines at that time. Mathematical logic was initially not only developed exclusively in order to analyze or to solve foundational problems in mathematics, as varied and broader aims were conceived in very different contexts. Gradually, some aspects of formal logic turned into the discipline today known as symbolic or mathematical logic.

The development of modern abstract mathematics (emancipated from quantity and geometrical forms) led to acceptance of logical relations also as mathematical objects. Thus, from this development the idea emerged of investigating the *mathematical structure* of logical relations, logical operators and more in general, of deductive reasoning. In the beginning of

---

[1] See, v.g., Lorenz (1984).

this development geometry played a decisive role. The principle of duality in projective geometry formulated in the first half of the 19th Century, is a good example (see Nagel **1939**, pp. 184 ff.). This principle, that motivated the principle of duality in the algebra of logic, suggested some sort of independence of the truth of a theorem from its content, some idea of 'formal truth' and the use of schematic expressions applicable to different objects is behind this principle. Traces of the notion of symbolic knowledge can already be found here.

The publication in 1879 of Frege's *Begriffsschrift* is traditionally regarded as a landmark in the history of logic. According to this view, the algebra of logic and Frege's logic have been put quite apart one from the other as different (and sometimes diverging) movements in the history of mathematical logic. Indeed, this was the basis for the differentiation between two main traditions and methodologies, the - so called-tradition of logic as calculus and logic as universal language. I will try to draw attention to the fact that Frege's approach exhibits - even though contrary to many of his own statements - points in common with the algebraic tradition in logic which are related to the idea of symbolic knowledge.

Something that went unnoticed after the rash development of symbolic logic in the 20th Century is that *both* the algebraists and Frege explicitly introduced representations of logic relations and operations with symbolic manipulations as an essential feature. These coincidences can be explained through the aid of the notion of symbolic knowledge in the case of the algebra of logic. The main question in this context can be put in the following words: what remained of the tradition of symbolic knowledge in Frege's foundational program? The answer to this question should reveal the epistemological aspects of Frege's conceptual script (Frege's symbolism as an epistemological tool) and will be connected with his ideas concerning mathematical knowledge.

1. Symbolic knowledge

Leibniz (1646-1716) introduced the idea of symbolic knowledge (*cogitatio caeca* or *cogitatio symbolica*) in his work in order to draw a fundamental distinction between forms of cognitive representations. Roughly speaking, it can be described as knowledge obtained by means of a semiotic structure of some kind and more precisely, Leibniz opposed it to intuitive knowledge. The locus classicus where the expression 'symbolic knowledge' appears is Leibniz's "Meditationes de cogitationes, veritate et ideis" from 1684 (see A VI 4, 587-588; GP IV, 423). Through this notion, Leibniz aimed at a justification of the epistemological use of calculi and artificial languages, that is, the use of calculi and artificial languages as a tool to gain new knowledge.

The resort to symbols arises, in first place, because of the limitations of human thinking in relation to the representation of certain objects. Leibniz seems to have taken this idea from the development of the algebra of his time and in connection with his own contributions to mathematics. We use the symbol or numeral '1000' to represent simultaneously one thousand units, or, using an example taken from Leibniz himself, a kiliogon, a polygon of a thousand sides, cannot be represented as a geometrical figure, so that a symbol to refer to it is needed. In second place, there are some notions that can only be represented by symbols. In this sense, symbolic knowledge is opposed to intuitive knowledge. This idea of symbolic knowledge should be understood in the context of the Leibnizian programs of both an *ars combinatoria* and of a *characteristica universalis*. The latter was conceived as a universal language, a scientific notation and a method for discovery or proof. It is in the *characteristica* that calculi can be constructed

The idea of symbolic knowledge is *pragmatic* in essence. It should be placed in the context of a semiotic perspective, and it does not involve only a semantic purpose. When using symbolic systems to gain new knowledge, semantics is not in the forefront. With the introduction of this notion of symbolic knowledge an important methodological innovation was achieved: the knowledge obtained through *symbolic manipulation*, produced in the form of calculi, has a prominent position in the whole structure of human knowledge. In this manipulation, symbols are seen as objects independently of their meaning. This feature leads to the idea of an 'operative symbolism' - opposed to an 'ontological symbolism', according to which the represented object is entirely independent from symbolism itself.[2] Moreover, symbolic systems provide proof procedures and decision methods. Proof is then understood as calculation in a symbolic system (see the preface to the general science, *Science générale*, from 1677, especially C 155).

Symbolic knowledge is also related in a critical sense to *concept formation*. One of the more important epistemological features of symbolic knowledge, already present in Leibniz, consists in introducing calculi with symbols without an intended reference for 'imaginable' objects, that cannot be grasped by sensible intuition. Although the reference of such symbols can be understood as 'fictitious' entities, they play an essential epistemological role in calculi: It is by means of them that an authentic new knowledge is obtained. A 'constitutive' aspect of symbolic knowledge has thus been asserted (s. Krämer **1992**). This would be the case of Leibniz's infinitesimal calculus and differential equations, where symbols are introduced without any denotative function, but in order to solve mathematical problems through a calculus. An example is the notion of infinitesimal as a "fiction bien fondée" (well founded fiction).

The notion of symbolic knowledge initiated a tradition in the methodology of formal sciences. After Leibniz other philosophers and

---

[2] See Krämer **1997**.

scientists of the 18th Century developed this notion in different directions - Christian Wolff and Johann Lambert among others. The contributions of Lambert are noteworthy in the context of the present discussion. Lambert introduced the idea of diagram and scheme (called by him *emblemata*) as a tool for symbolic knowledge. Their function consists in providing a natural and perceptual image of a relation between concepts. In this way a certain *structural resemblance* between the semiotic system and the conceptual system is achieved. As a consequence, the surrogative aspect of symbolic knowledge is stressed. Lambert developed his conception in the third part, "Semiotik", of his *Neues Organon* from 1764. This direction in symbolic knowledge leads to diagrammatic reasoning, which diverges in many aspects from Leibniz's idea of a *cogitatio caeca* and will not be discussed in this paper.

The main features of symbolic knowledge can be summarized as follows:

1. Symbolic systems are *physical systems* obeying operational rules. They can consist of figures, graphic signs, letters of the alphabet, etc.

2. Symbolic knowledge presupposes a *representational function* of symbolic systems. Representation must be understood here in the sense of mappings or morphism from a structure to another, allowing what is called *surrogative* reasoning.

3. Symbolic knowledge is knowledge of *formal structures* and their properties. By means of abstraction formal structures are determined and their properties can be analyzed.

4. Regarding their relevance for knowledge, symbolic systems are *meaning independent*. In this way, their formal properties can be analyzed. Besides, they can admit different interpretations.

5. Symbolic knowledge have an *instrumental* function. Symbolic systems are tools for obtaining knowledge and providing evidence *ad oculos* and decision tests.

6. Symbolic knowledge has a psycho-technical function, as long as it simplifies cognitive operations.

Furthermore, it is important to note the already mentioned opposition between symbolic and intuitive knowledge. Symbolic knowledge is obtained by means of a semiotic structure. This is what has been called *operative symbolism*: The symbolic structures "produce" the represented entities or features of them, so that the symbolism is in some sense *prior* to them and it does not have a merely representational function. This feature, albeit important, will not play an essential role in this paper. For the purposes of the following exposition, it is possible to isolate two basic ways of producing knowledge through a symbolic system:

(a) by manipulation of its symbols according to rules (this way would be knowledge by formal calculus in the stricter sense),

(b) by application of the symbolic system to a new domain, so that new properties of the domain can be known.

In the last case knowledge of formal structures is involved and it could be possible to speak of 'structural knowledge'. Both ways can be found in logic and mathematical research in the 18th and 19th Centuries, so that it makes sense to speak of a "tradition of symbolic knowledge". In it, however, the very notion of symbolic knowledge was discussed on very few occasions - even Leibniz's original ideas on the subject were unknown to many authors of this period.

2. Symbolic Knowledge in Boole´s algebra of logic

Even if Boole was not the first to attempt a mathematical treatment of logic, he is regarded as one of the founding fathers of symbolic logic, and in fact it can be said that he was the first in a continuous development of the subject. Boole's algebra of logic emerged from the new approach in algebra in Great Britain at the beginning of the 19th Century. The idea of symbolic knowledge did not appear explicitly in this movement. However, it was presupposed in the methodology of English algebraists. At the beginning of the 19th Century, the algebraic means of expression were increased, so that in mathematics symbols were written and manipulated without always keeping in mind the objects denoted. Notions such as "impossible quantities" and "impossible numbers" raised conceptual difficulties, so that the operating processes turned to be more important than the mere calculus. This English school originated in Cambridge, when Charles Babbage, John F. W. Herschel and George Peacock formed the Analytical Society in around 1812. They aimed to reform research in mathematics. For example, they forced the adoption of Leibnizian script for infinitesimal calculus in Cambridge, and imported from France new trends in mathematics.

In his *Treatise on Algebra*, Peacock conceived of algebra as a system of operations based on the faculties of the mind. These faculties made the laws of symbolical algebra necessary truths. In this context, Peacock stated the following "principle of the permanence of equivalent forms":

> Whatever form is algebraically equivalent to another when expressed in general symbols, must

continue to be equivalent, whatever those symbols denote.³

This principle means that the equivalence of two algebraic symbols (equivalence expressed by an equation) is independent of the interpretation assigned to the symbols. That is the reason why the principle refers to "general symbols", that is to variables without a fixed domain. The idea underlying this principle is that the equivalence is asserted by virtue of the properties of the symbols (expressed by postulates or definitions). For example, the equation

$$x(y+z) = xy + xz,$$

expressing the distributivity of the product related to the sum, depends of the postulates ruling on both operations without regarding the objects referred by these operations (numbers, segments, etc.).

A consequence of this principle is the distinction between 'arithmetical algebra' (dealing with numbers) and 'symbolical algebra' (as a mere abstract calculus). After Peacock, the conditions for a calculus of operations were studied. The Scottish mathematician Duncan Gregory (Boole's teacher) defined symbolical algebra as "the science which treats of the combination of operations defined not by their nature, that is, by what they are or what they do, but by the laws of combination to which they are subject" (Gregory **1840**, p. 208). Peacock's treatise influenced also Augustus De Morgan. In his *Trigonometry and Double Algebra* (from 1849), De Morgan argued that a "symbolic calculus" could be constructed on the basis of arbitrary symbols and a set of principles under which these symbols could be manipulated.

Boole's first work was devoted to the method of separation of symbols. He noticed the independence of the symbolical algebra from the notion of quantity and interpreted the principle of permanence as a principle about the *independence* of the calculus from its interpretations. In his book *The Mathematical Analysis of Logic,* published in 1847, Boole applied symbolical algebra to the field of logic, and, in accordance with the principle of the permanence of forms, he formulated the idea that the analysis of the laws of combination of symbols is independent from their interpretation:

> They who are acquainted with the present state of the theory of Symbolic Algebra, are aware, that the validity of the processes of analysis does not depend upon the interpretation of the symbols which are employed, but solely upon the laws of their combination. Every system of interpretation which does not affect the truth of the relations supposed, is equally admissible, and it is thus that

---

³ Peacock **1834**, p. 198.

> the same process may, under one scheme of interpretation, represent the solution of a question on the properties of numbers, under another, that of a geometrical problem, and under a third, that of a problem of dynamics or optics. This principle is indeed of fundamental importance.[4]

This principle was the very basis for the construction of a logical calculus:

> We might justly assign it [the former principle] as the definitive character of a true Calculus, that it is a method resting upon the employment of Symbols, whose laws of combination are known and general, and whose results admit of a consistent interpretation [...] It is upon the foundation of this general principle, that I purpose to establish the Calculus of Logic.[5]

In this way, the deductive inference could be represented by means of a mathematical structure:

> Every logical proposition [...] will be found to be capable of exact and rigorous expression [...] Every process will represent deduction, every mathematical consequence will express a logical inference.[6]

In his later book, *The Laws of Thought*, from 1854, Boole gave the name of 'Symbolical Reasoning' to this method. According to it he intermediate steps in formal processes that remain do not have an interpretation:

> [...] the validity of a conclusion arrived at by any symbolical process of reasoning, does not depend upon our ability to interpret the formal results which have presented themselves in the different stages of the investigation.[7]

So, intermediate steps are 'blind reasoning'. This "general method in logic" contains three main stages:

---

[4] Boole **1847**, p. 3.
[5] Boole **1847**, p. 4.
[6] Boole **1847**, p. 6.
[7] Boole **1854**, p. 67.

> The conditions of valid reasoning, by the aid of symbols, are
>
> 1st, That a fixed interpretation be assigned to the symbols employed in the expression of the data; and that the laws of the combination of those symbols be correctly determined from that interpretation.
>
> 2nd, That the formal processes of solution or demonstration be conducted throughout in obedience to all the laws determined as above, without regard to the question of the interpretability of the particular results obtained.
>
> 3rd, That the final result be interpretable in form, and that it be actually interpreted in accordance with that system of interpretation which has been employed in the expression of the data.[8]

This methodology of Boole's symbolical reasoning is exactly a specific form of symbolic knowledge, as described above. The second condition shows clearly Boole's (implicit) idea of symbolic knowledge: Boole's symbolic logic presupposes an 'operative symbolism, which is regarded, in a *pragmatic* turn, as an 'instrument of reasoning'.

Thus, this 'symbolical reasoning' constitutes the background of Boole's algebra of logic constructed in order to solve logical problems, such as the validity of an argument. In the first formulation of the system, the basic elements of Boole's algebra are "elective symbols": x, y, z, etc., the symbol 1 ("the universe") and the operations: +, ×, −. The algebra obeys the laws of commutativity and associativity (for + and −), distributivity (between + and ×) and inversion (for −). The idempotence of + and − (called 'index law' by Boole) was a distinctive feature of this algebra (see Boole **1847**, pp. 16 ff.)

According to this algebra, the categorical propositions of the traditional syllogistic are represented by means of equations in the following way

A: All Xs are Ys	---------->	$x(1 - y) = 0$
E: No Xs are Ys	---------->	$xy = 0$
I: Some Xs are Ys	---------->	$v = xy$
O: Some Xs are not Ys	---------->	$v = x(1 - y)$

This representation depends of the algebraic means available. The symbol v is used as an indefinite factor and express a rough idea of the existential quantification. (The problems related to this symbolic representation will not

---

[8] Boole **1854**, p. 68.

be discussed.) So, the *modus barbara* (under the schema 'All Ys are Xs, All Zs are Ys. Therefore All Zs are Xs') is represented as

$$y(1-x) = 0$$
$$z(1-y) = 0$$
$$\overline{z(1-x) = 0}^9$$

The validity of this figure is justified by an algebraic proof consisting in a chain of equations.

In the case of the application of the algebra to propositional logic ('secondary propositions' in Boole's terminology) another example is the *modus ponens*, formulated by Boole as 'X → Y is true, X is true. Therefore Y is true' is represented as:

$$x(1-y) = 0$$
$$x = 1$$
$$\overline{1-y = 0}$$

The solution to the problem of determining the validity of this scheme is given by the series of equations

1) $x(1-y) = 0$
2) $x = 1$
3) $1(1-y) = 0$ (1, 2 substitution)
4) $1-y = 0$

Thus, the representation of propositions is made according the proper solutions of logical problems, which are solved in a purely "computational" manner, without considering the real meaning of the expressions, in a "blind" way, so to say, and above all in a more simple way. In a posthumous paper, written after *The Laws of Thought*, Boole stated:

> The advantage I conceive to be that when we have established ... our right to the employement of a system whose laws are in every respect coincident with those of Logic but whose ideas are more simple we are led by easier steps of suggestion to the constructive development of the science.[10]

---

[9] Here note should be taken of the special form adopted by Boole for *modus ponens* and other propositional valid forms, in which the truth is predicated of the sentences. I will not discuss this here.
[10] Boole **1997**, p. 94.

So, there are pragmatic reasons for using symbolic algebra in logic.

Moreover, Boole's algebra of logic constitutes a clear case of *surrogative* reasoning: the algebraic conception of logical operations leads to an algebraic *representation* of deductive procedures and the problem of the validity of arguments is solved algebraically. For example the element 0 is introduced in the calculus as a consequence of the algebraic structure, as the dual of 1: given $xy = x$, it follows that $y = 1$, so that $x(1-y) = 0$ holds. The methods and resources depend on the algebraic system. In this point Boole's conception agrees with Leibniz's ideas, even if they do not exercise direct influence upon him (see Grattan-Guinness **1997**, p. xliii).

At the same time, Boole established his algebra as the mathematical structure of deductive reasoning and not as a mere device for solving logical problems. This approach was philosophically motivated. Boole was convinced that this structure was analogous to the structure of human mind. At the very beginning of his *Investigations*, Boole declared that the aim of the book was "to investigate the fundamental laws of those operations of the mind by which reasoning is performed." (Boole **1854**, p. 1) As a result of this investigation a foundation for the "science of Logic" could be found. The fundamental laws of the mind were those of algebra:

> There is not only a close analogy between the operations of the mind in general reasoning and its operations in the particular science of Algebra, but there is to a considerable extent an exact agreement in the laws by which the two classes of operations are conducted.[11]

This position was generally understood as a *psychologistic* foundation of both logic and algebra: the algebra of logic should be a 'mathematical psychology'. Of course, it is evident that Boole did not have the purpose of reflecting how human beings in fact reason. As he pointed out in the final chapter of the *Investigations*, in the actual processes of reasoning some "interferences" with the "laws of right reasoning" take place (see Boole **1854**, p. 409). So, the proper "laws of reasoning" are not the laws of the actual reasoning of individual minds. In addition, Boole made no specific statement about how he understood the quite broad notion of mind. It should be taken into account that for Boole the laws of the mind could not be known by observation of individual minds (Boole **1854**, p. 4).

In any case, Boole's psychologism is only one side of the ideas behind the algebra of logic, and Boole's words suggest that he was thinking of a *common structure* of the operation in the mind and in the symbolic system. Scientific research is for Boole based on the study of relations and

---

[11] Boole **1854**, p. 6.

operations, without taking into account the underlying nature of the relations and operations involved. As Boole states at the beginning of chapter III of the *Laws of Thought*,

> The object of science, properly so called, is the knowledge of laws and relations. To be able to distinguish what is essential to this end, from what is accidentally associated with it, is one of the most important conditions of scientific progress.[12]

The algebraic symbolism reveals more accurately than ordinary language the structural features of scientific objects and relations.[13]

3. The case of Ernst Schröder: algebra of logic and pasigraphy

The idea of symbolic knowledge is also present in contributions of Ernst Schröder to algebra and logic. Ernst Schröder (1841 –1902) was the main representative of the algebra of logic in Germany, as it had been conceived by Boole, and he also developed and systematized the logic of relations created by Charles S. Peirce. His main work is the *Lections on the Algebra of Logic* (*Vorlesungen über die Algebra der Logik*), in three volumes.[14]

We can divide Schröder's work in formal algebra and logic in three stages: (1) the discussion of a program for an absolute algebra, (2) further developments and systematization of Boole's algebra of logic, (3) further development and systematization of Peirce's algebra of relatives.

Independently from the symbolical algebraists in England, Schröder developed his ideas of formal algebra. In 1873 he published his *Lehrbuch der Arithmetik und Algebra* (*Textbook of Arithmetic and Algebra*), in which he characterized *formal algebra* as "those investigations on the laws of algebraic operations [...] that refer to nothing but general numbers in an unlimited number field (*Zahlgebiet*) without making any presuppositions about its nature" (Schröder **1873**, p. 233). He defined pure mathematics as the "science of number", but he did not associate number with quantities and he did not presupposed that a domain of numbers should be restricted to mathematics. One year later he considered examples of "domain of numbers" in this general sense could be "proper names, concepts, judgements, algorithms, numbers, symbols for dimensions and operations, points and systems of points, quantities of substances" (Schröder **1874**, p. 3).

---

[12] Boole **1854**, p. 39.
[13] Gerard Bornet has defended here a certain form of structuralism in Boole. See Bornet **1997**.
[14] The first volume appeared in 1890, the second in 1891. The third volume is divided in two parts. The first appeared in 1895, the second was published posthumously in 1905. More biographical data on Schröder and an account of his contributions to logic can be found in Peckhaus **2004**.

And he refers to "symbolic operations", that are applied to numbers in this general sense.

Figure 1

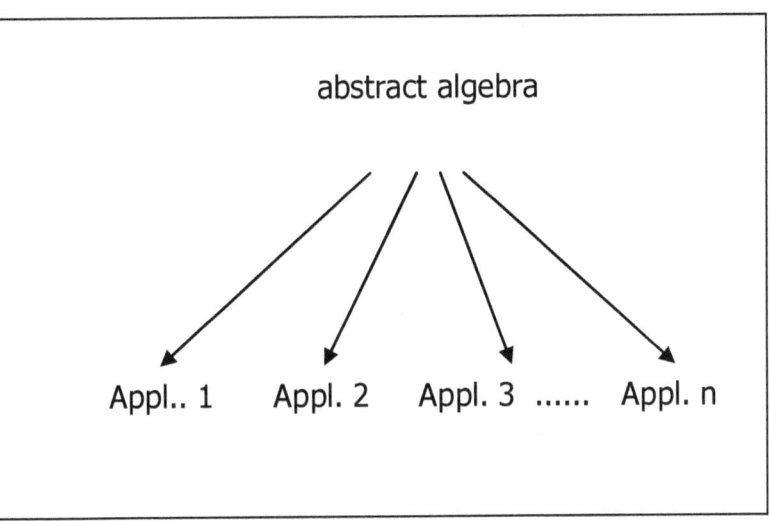

Schröder stressed the importance of symbolic manipulation in investigating logic and algebraic properties. This symbolic manipulation could only be achieved in an universal scientific language. In a short autobiographical sketch, published in 1901, Schröder evaluated his own contributions to logic and claimed that his aim was

> to make the logic a computational [*rechnerisch*] discipline [...] In this way, it would be possible to prepare the ground for an universal scientific language that presents itself absolutely different from the linguistic attempts à la Volapük, more as a language of signs [*Zeichensprache*] as a phonetic language [*Lautsprache*].[15]

Thus, symbolic systems played the role of both calculi and scientific languages.

Schröder devoted the introduction to volume I of the *Vorlesungen* to clarifying his point of view concerning logic, symbolic language and

---

[15] Schröder **1901**.

calculus. He sketches a semiotic foundation for logic. The object of logic for Schröder was thinking (*Denken*), and its final goal was the achievement of knowledge (see Schröder **1890**, p. 1). This thinking, "reduced to its strictest expression", is represented as a calculus (Schröder **1890**, p. 10), and any deduction copes with his more difficult tasks *by means of computation* (*rechnerisch*). In this sense, deduction "can not refrain from the powerful help of perception", which is the observation of symbols (*loc. cit.*). According to Schröder, the importance of symbols and language in the exact sciences is indebted to Trendelenburg's paper on Leibniz (Trendelenburg **1867**)[16]:

> These sciences tend to shift the difficulties in the study of *things* [...] on to the study of their signs, which are always available to the researcher and can be handled with incomparable easiness.[17]

In this context, Schröder refers to Leibniz's ideas about the role of language and symbolism in our knowledge, mainly with relation to objects or facts that cannot be grasped intuitively, as happens in Mathematics and Physics. He quotes several passages, and applies to representations (*Vorstellungen* - a word with Kantian echoes) Leibniz's distinction between intuitive and symbolic knowledge (Schröder **1890**, p. 41). Symbolic representations are needed in the event of a lack of intuitive objects. Symbolic representations are *mediate* representations.[18]

Now, the problem of the justification of symbolic manipulation led Schröder, in relation with his formal algebra, to what he called the "axiom of the inherence of signs". This states that

> in all our arguments and inferences the signs inhere in our memory – and even more on the paper [...] Without this principle [...] every deduction would indeed be illusory, since every deduction begins when [...] the investigations of the things has made room for the investigation of their signs.[19]

Two main features of symbolic systems occur in this text: first, that symbols are perceptible objects, and second that symbols play a surrogative role.

---

[16] Trendelenburg's paper on Leibniz's *ars characteristica* was very important for spreading the idea of a universal scientific language among German mathematicians and philosophers in the 19th Century.
[17] Schröder **1890**, p. 40.
[18] Schröder mentions as an example some facts from the electrodynamical theory of light, as it was formulated by Maxwell and H. Hertz.
[19] Schröder **1873**, pp. 16 f.

His original program of a formal algebra included four tasks for it in his *Textbook* (see Schröder **1873**, p. 294), which divided it in two main parts: the first one would consist in presenting and defining all operators for "numbers" (in an abstract way) by stipulations or postulates (in the form of equations or inclusions) and also the rules that serve to obtain conclusions from premises. The second part would consist in determining the domains of numbers that can be constructed by the operations defined in the first part and in providing interpretations or models for the algebras. In general, the consideration of formal algebra, together with their applications, is called by Schröder *absolute algebra*, a *general* theory of connections. Logic should be an application of formal algebra, so it would belong to absolute algebra. We face here a kind of structuralistic conception of algebra and logic. It is important to stress at this point that Schröder took logic and its properties as an algebraic issue. He did not aim to develop algebraic methods for solving logical problems but to construct an "algebra of logic", that is, to investigate the algebraic structure of logic.

We are facing here an explicit elucidation of the nature of logic through structural principles. Thus, logic is subordinate to algebra. As Risto Vilkko suggested, Schröder's algebra of logic implies a *structural* theory of logic (see Vilkko **2002**, p. 107). It means that logical knowledge is knowledge of its algebraic structure and this knowledge is possible by virtue of symbolic knowledge, as defined earlier.

The algebra of relatives - developed *in extenso* in vol. III of the *Vorlesungen* - provided a more general framework for his program of an abstract algebra. He conceived this algebra of relatives as structural theory applicable to an unlimited number of domains. In fact he applied it to Dedekind's chain-theory and Cantor's set theory. He uses it, therefore, as a tool, an instrument to present this result on a "logically computational base" ("logisch rechnerische Basis"), as he wrote in a letter to Felix Klein one year later.

In relation to this interpretation of Dedekind's chain-theory into the algebra of relatives, Schröder stressed explicitly the pragmatic function of the later, and pointed out some remarkable features of the algebraic representation (Schröder **1895**, p. 352). (1) The representation is more general, in the sense that the symbolic structure has a broader scope and range, so that it can be applied to different domains. (2) 'Shortcuts' (*Abkürzungen*) can be carried out in the proofs, that is, compared with ordinary language or other symbolisms proofs can be represented in a shorter way. (3) The notation has a greater expressiveness. ("As can be seen our method of script is more expressive", Schröder **1895**, p. 353.) So, a greater number of structural distinctions is possible. These features place Schröder's idea of the algebra of logic within the tradition of symbolic knowledge. We face here many of the essential notes of symbolic logic mentioned in section 2. The generality and expressiveness are in connection with the knowledge of formal structures, whose formal properties can be applied to different fields. The representation of proofs in an abbreviated, concise and more comprehensive way providing an easier symbolic manipulation implies 'blind' procedures for gaining knowledge.

4. Algebra of logic and symbolic knowledge: some preliminary conclusions

From the examination of the ideas underlying Boole´s and Schröder´s algebra of logic, it can be concluded that the two ways of obtaining knowledge through symbolic systems indicated at the end of section 2 are fulfilled in the algebra of logic. That is, new results can be obtained by symbolic manipulation and symbolic structures can be applied to different domains. Furthermore, these more specific conclusions can be drawn.

(1) The algebraic formulation of logic plays a more pragmatic than semantic role, namely the solution of logical problems. As it was observed in the preceeding sections, this fact is present already in Boole´s *Laws of Thought* but above all in Schröder´s work. However, in the case of Boole his thesis of the mathematical structure of the "laws of the mind" suggests a justification of algebraic symbolism beyond its practical function in solving problems. This can be interpreted as a withdrawal from symbolic knowledge in its strictest sense.

(2) Boole solves logical problems through "computations" in algebra. However, compared with the preceding attempts at logical calculi in the 18th Century, an important difference can be noticed. Boole devised an *algebraic structure* for logic, so that a whole new perspective for the analysis of logic is opened up. Algebraic properties can be ascribed to logical notions. This point of view is continued and deepened by Schröder, as he makes the structure more explicit through the idea of an abstract algebra including abstract operations.

Thus, in the evolution of the algebra of logic it can be perceived a shift both in interests and goals. The research is first focused on the construction of a calculus, a *computation*, mathematically accurate for solving logical problems, but afterwards it is led to the determination of the algebraic properties characterizing the mathematical *structure* of deductive inference. In both stages, features of symbolic knowledge – as characterized above – are present.

5. Frege's conceptual script

It was not difficult to make a connection between Boole´s and Schröder´s algebra of logic and the tradition of symbolic knowledge. If we now focus on Frege's well known contributions to mathematical logic, the main question concerning the aims of this paper can be formulated in the following words: What remained (if anything) of the tradition of symbolic knowledge in Frege's foundational program? The answer to this question should reveal the epistemological aspects of Frege's conceptual script (that is, Frege's symbolism as a tool for mathematical knowledge), and Frege's epistemology should be discussed. In order to do that his methodology of analysis and the role of definitions in his systems will be taken into account. It will be then argued that his ideas on concept formation based on the analysis of judgeable contents are clearly distinguished from the methodology of symbolic knowledge.

Gottlob Frege (1849-1925) introduced in *Begriffsschrift* from 1879 his logical system in order to found arithmetic on purely logical concepts. This logical system was absolutely original in many respects, and it can be easily interpreted as predicate or quantificational logic in the current sense. Because of this system he is undoubtedly counted among the founding fathers of mathematical logic. Frege formulated the system in a new and totally unusual symbolic system, which included lines, and strokes arranged in a two-dimensional form. This symbolic system was for Frege a '*Begriffsschrift*', that is, a conceptual script.

There is no doubt that *prima facie* Frege's conceptual script is intended to produce knowledge in the first of the ways mentioned above, that is, knowledge obtained by symbolic manipulation. This way is connected with Frege's idea of *proof*. However, it can be argued that the conceptual script was also conceived to represent formal structures. This representational side has in the case of Frege the following main features: (i) there is only one structure (the world) to be directly represented, (ii) it is an *ontological* representation: it represents basic components of reality. As a result the tension - already mentioned with relation to the algebra of logic- between *calculus* and *representation* can be found also in the case of Frege's conceptual script. This has been expressed traditionally by saying that Frege's conceptual script is conceived as a universal language.

Through his artificial language, Frege was able to accurately express his own ideas on the nature of logic and mathematics. The whole Fregean foundational program has as an essential medium or tool the conceptual script. In a paper in which Frege compared Peano's symbolism with his own, he described the motivation in developing conceptual script and stressed the importance of conceptual script for his research:

> I became aware of the need for a conceptual script when I was looking for the fundamental principles or axioms upon which the whole of mathematics rests. Only after this question is answered can it be

hoped to trace successfully the springs of knowledge upon which this science thrives.[20]

Some years later, Frege wrote to Jourdain: "My concern with the latter [the conceptual script] compelled me in turn to give more exact formulation of the fundamental concepts of arithmetic" (Frege to Jourdan 23/09/1902, Frege **1980**, p. 73). So, by means of conceptual script, it is possible for him to express and to accurately manipulate the basic notions for constructing arithmetic, as can be read in a short posthumous fragment:

> It is almost all tied up with the concept script, a concept construed as a function, a relation as a function of two arguments. the extension of a concept or class is not the primary thing for me. unsaturatedness both in the case of concepts and of functions. the true nature of concept and function recognized.[21]

All these statements undoubtedly stress the importance of symbolism in Frege's foundational program. It is generally known that according to him conceptual thinking and ordinary language were in a special relationship. Frege considered ordinary language was inadequate for this purpose because of its looseness, vagueness and ambiguity; it is not reliable and may lead to error. As Frege stated, "language proves to be deficient" (Frege **1882a**, p. 84). To avoid these deficiencies of ordinary language Frege created an artificial language (a 'written language' in opposition to 'spoken languages'), which he characterized as a 'Begriffsschrift', a conceptual script.

In the Preface of his fundamental work on the subject, Frege stated:

> This deficiency led me to the idea of the present conceptual script. Its first purpose, therefore, is to provide us with the most reliable test of the validity of a chain of inferences and to point out every presupposition that tries to sneak in unnoticed, so that its origin can be investigated.[22]

So, perspicuity, "logical perfection" and also brevity in the expressions and proofs were the aims of the conceptual script.

As expressed in the very title of this monograph, Frege was guided in the development of his conceptual script by the 'formula-languages'

---

[20] Frege **1897**, p. 235.
[21] Frege **1906**, p. 184.
[22] Frege **1879**, p. 6.

[*Formelsprachen*] already existing at that time in mathematics. Thus, it should be "modeled upon the formula-language of arithmetic" (*loc.cit.*). As he wrote later:

> I wanted to supplement the formula-language of mathematics with signs for logical relations so as to create a conceptual script which would make it possible to dispense with words in the course of a proof, and thus ensure the highest degree of rigour whilst at the same time making the proofs as brief as possible.[23]

In this language, symbols should be manipulated according to definite rules, so that it should achieve more perspicuity and precision than ordinary language, and every ambiguity could be banned. But, in addition, the symbolism "has a strict logical form from which the content cannot escape" (Frege **1882a**, p. 86). In other words, this language should be specially designed in order to express logical relations.

Some years later, in a letter to Hilbert, Frege insisted on the need for such 'mathematical sign language' [*Zeichensprache*] and described its origins in the imprecision of ordinary language:

> The natural way in which one arrives at a symbolism seems to me to be this: in conducting an investigation in words, one feels the broad, imperspicuous and imprecise character of word language to be an obstacle, and to remedy this, one creates a sign language [*Zeichensprache*] in which the investigation can be conducted in a more perspicuous way and with more precision.[24]

Now, Frege's conceptual script was conceived not only as a formal language to avoid logical errors and ambiguity, but also as a universal scientific language, which would "fill the gaps in the existing formula languages" and, as mentioned before, "connect their hitherto separated fields into a single domain" (Frege **1879**, p. 7). Thus, the conceptual script would follow the Leibnizian ideal of a scientific universal language (*lingua characterica*, as Frege called it following Trendelenburg). Frege enrolled himself in this Leibnizian tradition:

> In his scripts, Leibniz threw out such a profusion of seeds of ideas that in this respect he is virtually

---

[23] Frege **1882b**, Eng. transl.(1979) p. 47.
[24] Frege to Hilbert 1.10.1895, in Frege **1980**, p. 33.

in a class of his own. A number of these seeds were developed and brought to fruition within his own lifetime and with his collaboration, yet more were forgotten, then later discovered and developed further. This justifies the expectation that a great deal in his work that it is now to all appearance dead and buried will one day enjoy a resurrection. As part of this, I count an idea which Leibniz clung to throughout his life with the utmost tenacity, the idea of a *lingua characterica*, an idea which in his mind had the closest possible links with that of a *calculus ratiocinator*.[25]

To sum up, Frege´s conceptual script would serve as a universal formal language in which every logical law can be expressed accurately. On the basis of this script, Frege believed to he was well-placed to reconstruct the fundamental notions of arithmetic.

6. Frege and the algebraic tradition

Frege´s conceptual script was criticized and misunderstood by his contemporaries (Schröder included). This situation gave rise to a series of papers in which Frege attempted to explain his own ideas and to argue for them, showing the advantages of his conceptual script in relation with the algebra of logic. In this context, he characterized his symbolic script as a *language* and not as a mere calculus.

This controversy and Frege´s reaction motivated Jean van Heijenoort to draw in his seminal paper of 1967 two fundamental lines of thought in the history of modern logic: *logic as language* (exemplified by Frege's conceptual script) and *logic as calculus* (represented by the algebra of logic).[26] Specifically, van Heijenoort took this distinction from Frege´s own opposition, between *lingua characterica* and *calculus ratiocionator*, expressed in various papers, effectively outlining two different approaches in mathematical logic. Thus, he stated:

---

[25] Frege **1880/1881**, p. 9. This is not originally a Leibnizian expression; see the comments in Thiel **1965**, note 12, and by Günther Patzig in Frege **1986**, note 8. Following Wilhelm von Humboldt, Trendelenburg referred to the idea of a "Begriffsschrift" in which the structure of concepts can be accurately represented by means of the structure of signs (Trendelenburg **1867**, p. 4). Trendelenburg´s paper influenced also Frege in this respect too.

[26] This distinction is regarded as the "received view of the history of modern logic among the non-historians". See Peckhaus **2004**. To some extent, it corresponds to another distinction between two schools in modern logic: the algebra of logic, on the one hand, and mathematical logic and mathematical logic or "the logic of mathematicians" on the other. The distinction concerns the goals and the methodology employed in each case. Frege should be included in the second school, but he would not be the sole- or main - representative of it.

> I was trying, in fact, to create a 'lingua characterica' in the Leibnizian sense, not a mere 'calculus ratiocinator'.[27]

With the expression 'lingua characterica', Frege meant a language where the interpretation cannot be separated from the language itself, serving "to express a content", as Frege wrote. The expressions of the language are meaningful *ab initio*. His conceptual script was conceived not only as a formal language to avoid logical errors and ambiguity, but also as a *universal scientific language*, which would "fill the gaps in the existing formula languages" and "connect their hitherto separated fields into a single domain" (Frege **1879**, p. 7). On the contrary, a calculus was conceived only as a symbolic system with not fixed interpretation, and it was intended to be a formal representation of logic for solving logical problems. It must be taken into account that Frege wrote this comment as an answer to Schröder's criticism, who in turn disregarded Frege's system as a mere calculus (s. Schöder **1880**) and not as a *real Begriffsschrift* or as a "Pasigraphy", that is, an universal language. This opposition has different aspects. Frege's conception implies that in the language the problem of the variability of interpretation does not even arise, while for the algebraists the universe of discourse can be changed (see van Heijenoort **1967**). This idea was implicit in his characterization of quantification.

Frege critized Boole's logic by saying that "it deals solely with logical form, and not at all with the injecting of a content into this form" (Frege **1896**, p. 242).[28] What Frege did reject was the consideration of his conceptual script as a mere manipulation of void symbols without a content, as an "abstract logic":

> Right from the start I had in mind the *expression of a content* [*Ausdruck eines Inhaltes*]. What I am striving after is a lingua characterica in the first instance for mathematics, not a *calculus* restricted to pure logic.[29]

Frege regarded Boole's logical calculus as a technique [*Technik*] for resolving logical problems (s. *loc. cit.*). In this sense, he differentiated absolutely his conceptual script from Boolean logic:

---

[27] Frege **1883**, p. 89.
[28] With 'logical form', Frege means here the usual idea of a pure structure without content but not his own conception of formal theory (see Frege **1885**).
[29] Frege **1880/1881**, p. 12.

> ... my purpose was quite other than Boole's. I was not trying to present an abstract logic in formulas; I was trying to express contents in an exacter and more perspicuous manner than is possible in words, by using written symbols.[30]

Frege thought that there was more to logic than mere calculation. Again, Frege aimed at a contentual *Formelsprache*.

However, Frege did not always express himself negatively towards Boole's algebra of logic. On the contrary, he regarded "the divergences from Boole as improvements, by and large" (Frege **1897**, p. 242). It must be remembered that this conceptual script was a medium for Frege's logicist project. In the conceptual script the basic (logical) concepts should make it possible to define every arithmetical concept, and from the (purely logical) axioms and definitions every arithmetical theorem should follow.

7. Frege's conceptual script as calculus

From the preceding quotations it can be argued that Frege's position would at first sight rule out symbolic knowledge as part of his methodological tool-box (at least in its strictest sense). This is because his conceptual script cannot be conceived as a symbolic structure independent from a given domain, and thus applicable to different domains and open to possible extensions by means of the introduction of new (undefined) notions. However, this consequence can give rise to objections. In his paper on Peano's symbolism, Frege added further comments about his conceptual script:

> In Leibnizian terminology we can say: Boole's logic is a *calculus ratiocinator* but not a *lingua characterica* [...] whereas my conceptual script is both, with equal emphasis.[31]

So, Frege's conceptual script has two interpretations: as a calculus and as a language. In it is possible to represent logical propositions and to perform, on the basis of this representation, logical inferences in a computational way:

> In my conceptual script inference is conducted like a calculation [*nach Art einer Rechnung*]. I do not mean this in the narrow sense, as if it were subject to an algorithm the same as or similar to that of

---

[30] Frege **1883**, p. 89.
[31] Frege **1897**, p. 242.

> ordinary addition and multiplication, but only in the sense that there is an algorithm there at all [*daß überhaupt ein Algorithmus da ist*], i.e. a totality of rules which govern the transition from one sentence or from two sentences to a new one in such a way that nothing happens except in conformity with these rules.[32]

This language could yield a calculus, a 'mechanism' as Frege wrote to Hilbert:

> I would not want to regard such a mechanism as completely useless or harmful. On the contrary, I believe that it is necessary. The natural course of events seems to be as follows: what was originally saturated with thought hardens in time into a mechanism which partly relieves the scientist from having to think.[33]

The symbols of contentual language are transformed in the elements of a 'mechanism', a mechanical procedure, a calculus, which, contrary to Boole's position, does not represent 'thinking' in a creative sense.

In a late paper, Frege identified three sources of knowledge: sense perception, logic and the geometrical source (see Frege **1924/1925**). Because of the fact that Frege founded arithmetic on logic, arithmetical knowledge is to be identified with logical knowledge. Its origin is in the pure thinking, which in its turn is closely bound up with language (and language is here conceived in a general broadest sense, including symbolic systems in general). Language, Frege states, is something perceptible that is also necessary for thinking:

> Our thinking is closely bound up with language and thereby with the world of the senses. Perhaps our thinking is at first a form of speaking which then becomes an imaging of speech [...] Now we may of course also think in mathematical signs; yet even then thinking is tied up with what is perceptible to the senses.[34]

Frege refers here to the obvious fact that symbolic systems are constituted by sensible objects. Language and, more generally, symbolic

---

[32] Frege **1897**, p. 237.
[33] Frege to Hilbert, 1/10/1895, Frege **1980**, p. 33.
[34] Frege **1924/1925**, p. 269.

systems are sensible bases for thinking, they are conditions for thinking. This idea had been repeated by Frege earlier, for example in his letter to Hilbert dated October 1st., 1895 through the statement: "One can think also in symbols". Thinking can be made by symbols, and this is Leibniz's idea of *cogitatio symbolica*: symbols are an instrument for knowledge. Although the point is controversial (especially in this text from his late work), Frege means not ordinary language but symbolic systems like his conceptual script (or other 'universal scientific languages' of that time).

The system of strokes that constitutes the logical part of his conceptual script was designed by Frege in order to achieve (1) an accurate representation of logical facts, and (2) to provide an inference mechanism for deriving arithmetical theorems from logical axioms. This system of strokes has been described and analyzed on many occasions, and I do not aim to give a full account of it here.[35]

As it is known, the content stroke — applied to a letter A gives

—A,

stating that "the proposition that A" or " A is a propositional content". The judgement-stroke $|$, when applied to the content-stroke renders an expression like

⊢ A,

stating that "The proposition A is the case". Now, Frege introduced also the conditional stroke connecting two propositions in a *two-dimensional* way. Given two propositions —A and —B,

$$\begin{array}{c} \text{—A} \\ \text{—B} \end{array}$$

is a new proposition composed from the two propositions A and B, graphically represented with A as the "upper" proposition and B as the "lower" proposition. In section 5 of his 1879 book, Frege elucidates the conditional stroke in terms of the combination of truth-values of the propositions it connects (in fact, the possibility of being affirmed or denied, see Frege **1879**, § 5). So, the conditional stroke excludes the possibility of certain combination of the values of propositions and allows other combinations. It excludes the possibility of the upper proposition not to be the case and the lower proposition to be the case.

---

[35] A good summary of the system is given by Frege himself at the beginning of his paper from 1880/1881. A detailed exposition can be found in Appendix 3 of Beaney **1996**, and in Sullivan **2004**, section 2.

To this system of strokes Frege added furthermore another symbol, the negation stroke. When this symbol is applied to a propositional content —A, a new propositional content

 A

obtains, representing that the proposition A is not the case. With this two-dimensional system of strokes, Frege could express accurately every combination of possibilities of "being the case" or "not being the case" of a finite number of propositional contents.[36] Thus, he was able to express every "logical fact".

This rough and partial sketch of the conceptual script illustrates the fact that symbolic knowledge was implicitly one of the guiding ideas in its construction. The two-dimensionality of the conceptual script is an important feature of the conceptual script when we try to analyze it within the framework of symbolic knowledge. It is known that Frege constructed his symbolic language in a two-dimensional way in order to achieve a better understanding of logical relations. Frege's conditional stroke gave his symbolism its two-dimensional character.[37]

> The spatial relations of written symbols on a two-dimensional script surface can be employed in far more diverse ways to express inner relationships [innere Beziehungen] than the mere following and preceding in one-dimensional time, and this facilitates the apprehension of that to which we direct our attention. In fact, simple sequential ordering in no way corresponds to the diversity of logical relations through which thoughts are interconnected.[38]

There are different possible interpretations of this two-dimensional symbolism and its use. It can be interpreted in a mere *figurative* sense. According to this interpretation, implication is better represented with the antecedent *under* the consequent. However, other aspects are undoubtedly more important. The two-dimensionality plays an essential role in the computational side of the system. The proof constructions in the conceptual script follow specific graphic forms. So, the conceptual notation can be understood as a *diagrammatic* system providing symbolic knowledge in another sense.

---

[36] This property was characterized later as the functional completeness of the connectives of negation and conditional.
[37] This problem was discussed recently. See, for example, Macbeth **2005**.
[38] Frege **1882a**, p. 111, engl. transl., p. 87.

Frege introduced the rule of detachment (or *modus ponens*)

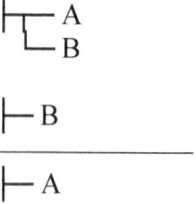

as the only deduction rule of his system and it is explicitly formulated in § 6 of Frege 1879. (As is known, the system contains other no explicit rules like substitution.) In this rule an axiom with the conditional stroke as main symbol can be the major premise and the "subordinate" or "lower" proposition of it as the minor premise. Therefore, the "upper" proposition can be deduced. By means of this quasi mechanical diagrammatic procedure, Frege sketches some kind of "normal form" for proofs in the conceptual script. Moreover, a procedure for proof search (to look for the premises for a theorem) is suggested in the same section of *Begriffsschrift*. Frege explains in detail how the symbols are manipulated in a purely blind way in the procedure of derivation of theorems from his logical axioms.

It can be argued that these features of Frege's conceptual script are the reason for Schröder to label it in his review of *Begriffsschrift* as a mere *calculus ratiocinator* and not as a language (see Schröder **1880**). If Frege's notions of predication and quantification, and also his ontological and semantic distinction between object and concept, are left aside a pure formal calculus for proving the validity of a large number of arguments obtains. Moreover, one of the reasons Frege had to disregard his conceptual script as a mere calculus was precisely that logical reasoning could not be isolated from the arithmetical content of his language.

8. Symbolic knowledge and analysis in Frege's conceptual script

At this point Frege's conception of arithmetical knowledge and its relation to the conceptual script is to be discussed. On many occasions, Frege described the mere symbol manipulation in a calculus as "dangerous" for the development of science. He gave two reasons for that. Firstly, the danger would lie in the impossibility of warranting the truth of the formulas inferred in a calculus. Secondly, calculi can paralyze creative thinking and prevent the enhancement of our knowledge. As Frege states in the mentioned letter to Hilbert:

> A mere mechanical operation with formulas is dangerous (1) for the truth of the results and (2) for the fruitfulness of the science. The first danger can probably be avoided almost entirely by making the system of signs logically perfect. As far as the second danger is concerned, science would come to a standstill if the mechanism of formulas were to become so rampant as to stifle all thought.[39]

With regard to the first danger, Frege is taking into account the possibility of some control test of the calculi like consistency proofs (that would make them 'logically perfect' – using Frege's own expression). The second danger, however, still remains: calculi are against the 'fruitfulness' of science. Moreover, Frege compared the 'calculization' of scientific theories with the process of lignification of trees:

> Where a tree lives and grows it must be soft and succulent. But if what was succulent did not in time turn into wood, the tree could nor reach a significant height. On the other hand, when all that was green has turned into wood, the tree ceases to grow.[40]

Thus, the use of calculi does not contribute to advancement and renewal of science, and so an idea of symbolic knowledge as it was characterized in section 2 should be not possible for Frege.

Frege's classification of aspects of human knowledge according to their respective sources was already mentioned. Frege distinguished three sources of human knowledge: sense perception, the geometrical source (some kind of intuition, providing us the notion of infinity) and the logical source of knowledge, by means of which arithmetical knowledge is achieved. This logical source was based on an analysis of the logical form underlying linguistic expressions, so that logical knowledge is in some sense *linguistic* knowledge. This conception was one of the roots of the *semantic tradition*: Linguistic analysis provided the way to obtain *a priori* knowledge.[41]

Therefore, the introduction of an arithmetical concept is the result of an analysis of the expressions where this concept is used until finding in them the logical notions necessary for the formulation of an accurate definition. This idea of linguistic analysis depended on the perspicuous and exact

---

[39] Frege to Hilbert, 1/10/1895, Frege **1980**, p. 33.
[40] Frege to Hilbert, 1/10/1895, Frege **1980**, p. 33.
[41] This is the idea developed, for example, in Coffa **1991**. As Coffa observed the semantic tradition in philosophy emerged from the supposition of the analyticity of mathematical truths (see Coffa **1991**, chap. 4).

expression of every logical notion, as mentioned in section 6. Again, for Frege ordinary language was imperfect to this end because of its vagueness. Moreover, the correctness of inferences drawn in ordinary language cannot be established, since "in [ordinary] language, logical relations are almost always only hinted at – left for guessing, not actually expressed." (Frege **1882a**, p. 85.)

Such analysis was only possible in a formal language like the conceptual script, designed in order to regiment ordinary language (German in his case).[42] Therefore, the conceptual script played, it could be said, a surrogative role with relation to ordinary language. Like in the case of Leibniz, ordinary language provided only a *negative* form of 'blind thinking', so that an artificial language had to be constructed in order to achieve a positive or genuine form of it. It can be discussed if from the semantic point of view, the conceptual script was essential or not. Notwithstanding, it was *pragmatically* essential in Frege's program. Only in it logical concepts and logic truths could be represented in an accurate way, and, furthermore, the systematization and development of arithmetic depended in fact from it.[43] These pragmatic features can be regarded as a heritage from the tradition of symbolic knowledge.

Frege was not mainly interested in the *formal* construction of arithmetic (that is, in terms of symbolic systems) but in the justification of mathematical knowledge. For him the problem concerned above all *mathematical content*, as in the case of Kant who rejected also a formal approach to mathematics. Nevertheless, contrary to Kant, he denied the synthetic character of arithmetical truths. Logicism was his solution to the problem of justifying arithmetical truths as analytical and a priori, *not depending on intuitions*. This is a point Frege's methodology also had in common with the tradition of symbolic knowledge. It is evident that because of his strong platonism, symbolism could not play a constitutive role in his program. So, an 'operative symbolism' as it was conceived in the tradition of symbolic knowledge, should be ruled out. In general, the auxiliary use of symbolism is independent of the philosophical position adopted about mathematical truth. Symbolism can be understood in different ways and it can represent different kind of entities (intuitions or concepts, for example). Now, Frege's methodology started out from a contentual analysis of concepts to seize the nature of logical notions, that should be expressed in the conceptual script.[44]

---

[42] See Frege's posthumous paper "Notes for Ludwig Darmstaedter" from 1919 (Frege **1979**, pp. 253-257). Due to its imperfection, ordinary language was an obstacle to foundational research.

[43] See Coffa **1991**, pp. 66 and 73. Coffa disregarded the role of the conceptual script for the semantic aims of Frege. But this is not the whole story. Frege could not carry out his program using ordinary language.

[44] The epistemological role of analysis in Frege is described within its historical context in Haaparanta **1988**.

Both this analysis and the conceptual script played a 'fruitful' role in arithmetic. This role depends on what is called Frege's 'priority principle'. In connection with his semantic 'context principle', it states that judgements (propositions) always precede their constitutive concepts in every science. As Frege wrote in his paper on Boole's logic:

> I start out from judgements and their contents, and not from concepts [...] I only allow the formation of concepts to proceed from judgements.[45]

In doing this he followed a perspective widespread in 19th Century German philosophy, originated in Kant. This perspective opposed not only to the algebraic Boolean approach, but also to the old tradition stemming from Aristotle and followed also by Leibniz. According to this tradition, concepts are the ultimate and independent units of analysis and synthesis, the building blocks in knowledge representation. In a letter from 1882a, Frege described this idea in the following words:

> I do not believe that concept formation can precede judgement because this would presuppose the independent existence of concepts, but I think of a concept as having arisen by decomposition from a judgeable content.[46]

There are different ways in which a judgeable content can be decomposed. In the same letter, Frege gives the example of the decomposition of the content '3>2'. In it we can regard either 2 or 3 as 'subjects' (in Frege's sense). In the former case, the concept is 'smaller than 3' in the latter 'greater that 2' (see loc. cit.).

Now, the priority principle introduces a *new* methodology for concept formation that reveals itself to be essential for Frege's logicism, because it allowed him to introduce arithmetical concepts on the basis of logical concepts. This introduction is provided by definitions depending on the idea of analysis of a judgeable content, and it is called the method of *definition by analysis* (see, among others, Ruffino **1991**, where this idea is explained by means of Frege's theory of sequences in the third part of the *Begriffsschrift*). New concepts are introduced through definition by analysis.

Consequently, the methodology for concept formation based on the analysis of judgeable contents can be also clearly distinguished from the methodology of symbolic knowledge sketched earlier. In the case of symbolic knowledge, new 'fruitful' concepts are introduced straightforwardly by means of new symbols in calculi, making possible the

---

[45] Frege **1880/1881**, p. 16.
[46] Letter to Marty 8/29/1882a, Frege **1980**, p. 101.

derivation of new results or theorems. These symbols can firstly refer to 'fictitious' objects and later it may happen that a structure including these objects can be determined as a model of the calculus. That is the case of Leibniz and the algebraists of the 19th Century. But these symbols for fictitious entities are introduced mainly in abstract algebraic systems to mathematical ends. It must be stressed, then, that in pure logical domains this situation could hardly arise, as logical symbols had of course no reference, and it was only their structure that was represented algebraically. Moreover, for the algebraic logicians mathematical and logical interpretations of abstract algebra were quite apart, and it made no sense to reduce one interpretation to the other.

On the contrary, Frege's priority principle takes for granted that symbolism has the function of *describing* an already given reality, and it is only a task of analysis of judgements to define concepts. In this case, analysis comes to be a method for gaining knowledge, an *ars inveniendi* of some kind, and it is the basis for the 'logical source' of *arithmetical knowledge*.[47] Arithmetical concepts are traced back to logical concepts. Of course, the idea is that 'logical concepts' – in Frege's sense- are enough to define arithmetical concepts. In *Begriffsschrift* this method is exemplified by the definition of the 'ancestral' in a relation (more specifically, the notions of 'x follows y in the sequence f,' see Frege **1879**, § 24 ff.).

10. Concluding remarks

In the preceding sections, I have intended to show how the tradition of symbolic knowledge was present in the basic ideas of some of the founding fathers of mathematical logic. As a conclusion it can be argued that the tradition of symbolic knowledge contributed essentially to the development of mathematical logic in its different trends.

The cases of Boole and Schröder seem to be rather straightforward in this respect. Boole´s 'symbolical reasoning' contains many essential features of symbolic knowledge, as shown in section 3. Furthermore, the idea of using symbolic structures as an epistemological tool was also pointed out in section 5. In the case of Schröder, it can be observed how symbolic structures are formulated in order to build a *general* formal language, his *pasigraphy*, to be applied to different fields.

The case of Frege required a more complex study. If Frege's conceptual script is analyzed in the framework of the tradition of symbolic knowledge, it reveals itself as a *scientific universal language,* that is, as a system of symbols including a "computational" procedure with no immediate relation

---

[47] Together with proofs in the conceptual script, this procedure leads to the whole plant from its seeds, following Frege´s analogy in *The Foundations of Arithmetic* (Frege **1884**, p. 100). Following Haaparanta **1988**, p. 81, the whole system is "a mirror of the forms of thought".

to ordinary language, and with the goal of representing logical objects, operators and facts. In this tradition, Frege follows Leibniz, not Lambert. Even if the stroke configurations of the conceptual script attempt to show some similarities at the conceptual level, they serve the purpose of expressing abstract relations and of making a calculus (formal deductions) possible.

When he conceived his conceptual script, Frege was aware of the different attempts at "symbolic reasoning" of his time, as can be seen from the papers he wrote immediately after the publication of *Begriffsschrift*. For many reasons, he considered these attempts inaccurate for his own foundational project.[48] However, his project shared with them the idea of symbolic manipulation and computational procedures. Frege was compelled to do that in order to give a precise account of what has to be counted as a proof or a definition in his system, and to express with absolute rigour its basic notions. In doing that, the proof of a theorem was performed "like a calculation"; he was influenced by the tradition of symbolic knowledge.

The underlying role played by the notion of symbolic knowledge in the development of mathematical logic can provide a new insight into the famous distinction between calculus and language in the history of mathematical logic. It can be suggested that both in Schröder's algebra of relatives and Frege's conceptual script the aim was to construct simultaneously a calculus *and* a language. So, it is possible to conceive a historical evolution in the second half of the 19th Century where the focus was shifted from the construction of calculi to the formulation of formal languages and formal theories in order to represent mathematical entities. Schröder, on one side, is an example of the idea of representing mathematical structures with general applicability. On the other side, for Frege symbolic systems express a content and formal theories represent logical facts.[49]

It could be argued that this general change of focus was due to the problem of determining the basic mathematical objects (sets, relations, functions, etc.) and the nature of these objects. In this evolution some features of formal languages that are related to the notion of symbolic knowledge lost importance. Anyway, the implication arrived at is that the distinction is not as clear cut as originally van Heijenoort (and later also Jaakko Hintikka) believed.

In the history of mathematical logic another evolution has taken place, in which the tradition of symbolic knowledge played a role. In its historical development the purely *computational* features of calculus gives way to its *structural* features: a calculus turns into a way to represent a structure. This fact can be confirmed easily in the evolution of the algebra of logic. The

---

[48] To distinguish clearly between symbols for mathematical and logical notions was one of the reasons Frege had.

[49] In the case of Schröder, evidence is provided in Peckhaus **2004**, pp. 597 ff.

situation of Frege is in this case more problematic. The structural features of the conceptual script are hidden by Frege's ideas concerning language and meaning (the representational relation cannot be investigated), and Frege stressed the computational properties of his symbolism. Thus, Frege seems to be behind the algebraists in this evolution.

References

Beaney, M. 1996. *Frege: Making Sense*. London, Duckworth.

Boole, G. 1847. *The Mathematical Analysis of Logic. Being an Essay Towards a Calculus of Deductive Reasoning.* Cambridge. Macmillan, Barclay and Macmillan

Boole, G. 1854. *An Investigation of The Laws of Thought, on which are Founded The Mathematical Theories of Logic And Probabilities.* London, Walton and Maberly.

Boole, G. 1997. *Selected Manuscripts on Logic and Its Philosophy*. Ed. by Ivor Grattan-Guinness and Gérard Bornet. Basel-Boston-Berlin, Birkhäuser.

Bornet, G. 1997. "Boole´s Psychologism as a Reception Problem". In Boole 1997, pp. xlviii-lxiv.

Coffa, A. 1991. *The Semantic Tradition from Kant to Carnap. To The Vienna Station.* Edited by Linda Wessels. Cambridge - New York, Cambridge University Press.

Esquisabel, O. M. & Legris, J. 2003. "Conocimiento simbólico y representación". In *Representación en ciencia y arte*, ed. by Leticia Minhot & Ana Testa. Córdoba (Argentina), Brujas - Universidad Nacional de Córdoba, pp. 233-243.

Frege, G. 1879. *Begriffschrift*. Halle, Louis Nebert. Reprinted in Angelelli, Ignacio (ed.). *Gottlob Frege. Begriffschrift und andere Aufsätze. Mit E. Husserls und H. Scholz´ Anmerkungen.* Darmstadt, Wissenchaftliche Buchgesellschaft, 1964. Tr. by S. Bauer-Mengelberg in *From Frege to Gödel. A Source Book in Mathematical Logic, 1879-1931*, ed. by Jean van Heijenoort, Cambridge (Mass.), Harvard University Press,1967, pp. 5-82.

Frege, G. 1880/1881. "Booles rechende Logik und die Begriffsschrift". Tr. as "Boole's logical Calculus and the Concept-script" in Frege 1979, pp.9-46.

Frege, G. 1882a. "Über die wissenschaftliche Berechtigung einer Begriffschrift". Tr. as "On The Scientific Justification of a Conceptual Script" in Frege 1972, pp. 83-89.

Frege, G. 1882b. "Booles logische Formelsprache und meine Begriffsschrift". Tr. as "Boole's logical Formula-language and my Concept-Script". In Frege 1979, pp. 47-52.

Frege, G. 1883. "Über den Zweck der Begriffsschrift". Tr. as "On The Aim of The Conceptual Script" in Frege 1972, pp. 90-100.

Frege, G. 1884. Die Grundlagen der Arithmetik. Breslau, Verlag von Wilhelm Koebner. Reprinted Hamburg, Felix Meiner, 1986.

Frege, G. 1885. "Über formale Theorien der Arithmetik". English translation "On Formal Theories of Arithmetik" in Frege 1984, pp. 112-121.

Frege, G. 1896. "Über die Begriffsschrift des Herrn Peano und meine eigene". Tr. as "On Mr. Peano's Conceptual Script and My Own" in Frege 1984, pp. 234-248.

Frege, G. 1906. "Was kann ich als Ergebnis meiner Arbeit ansehen?". Tr. as "What may I regard as the Result of my Work" in Frege 1979, p. 184.

Frege, G. 1924/1925. "Erkenntnisquellen der Mathematik und der mathematischen Naturwissenschaft". Tr. as "Sources of Knowledge of Mathematics and Mathematical Natural Sciences" in Frege 1979, p. 267-274.

Frege, G. 1972. *Conceptual Script and related articles*, comp. por Terrel Ward Bynum, Oxford, Oxford University Press, 1972.

Frege, G. 1979. *Posthumous Scripts*. ed. by Hans Hermes, Friedrich Kambartel and Friedrich Kaulbach, tr. by P. Long & R. White. Oxford, Blackwell.

Frege, G. 1980. *Philosophical and Mathematical Correspondence*, ed. by Gottfried Gabriel, Hans Hermes, Friedrich Kambartel, Christian Thiel and Albert Veraart, tr. by H. Kaal. Oxford, Blackwell, 1980.

Frege, G. 1984. *Collected Papers on Mathematics, Logic and Philosophy*, ed. by B. McGuinness, tr. by M. Black et al. Oxford, Blackwell.

Frege, G. 1986. *Logische Untersuchungen*, ed. Günther Patzig, 3rd ed., Göttingen, Vandenhoeck & Ruprecht.

Gabbay, D. M. & Woods, J. (eds.) 2004. *Handbook of The History of Logic. Vol. 3. The Rise of Modern Logic: From Leibniz to Frege*. Amsterdam, et al., Elsevier – North Holland.

Grattan-Guinness, I. 1997. "Boole's Quest for the Foundations of Logic". In Boole 1997, pp. xiii-xlvii.

Haaparanta, L. 1988. "Analysis as the Method of Logical Discovery: Some Remarks on Frege and Husserl". Synthese 77 (1988), pp. 73-97.

Krämer, S. 1992. "Symbolische Erkenntnis bei Leibniz". *Zeitschrift für philosophische Forschung* 46, pp. 173-180.

Krämer, S. 1997. "Kalküle als Repräsentation. Zur Genese des operativen Symbolismus in der Neuzeit". In H.-J. Rheinberger, M. Hagner & B. Wahring Schmidt (eds.), *Räume des Wissens: Repräsentation, Codierung, Spur*, Berlin, Akademie Verlag, pp.111-122.

Leibniz, G. W. A. *Sämtliche Schriften und Briefe*. Edited by the German Academy of Sciences in Berlín, Berlín since 1923.

Leibniz, G. W. GP. *Die Philosophische Schriften von Gottfried Wilhelm Leibniz*, ed. by Carl Immanuel Gerhardt, 7 vols., Berlin, Weidmannsche Buchandlung, 1875-1890.

Leibniz, G. W. C. *Opuscules et Fragments inédits de Leibniz. Extraits des manuscrits de la Bibliothèque royale de Hanovre*, ed. by Louis Couturat. Paris, Alcan, 1903.

Lorenz, K. 1984. "Kalkül". In *Enzyklopädie Philosophie und Wissenschaftstheorie* vol II, ed. by Jürgen Mitelstraß. Mannheim - Vienna - Zurich.

Macbeth, D. 2005. *Frege's Logic*. Cambridge (Mass.) - London, Harvard University Press.

Nagel, E. 1939. "The Formation of Modern Concepts of Formal Logic in the Development of Geometry". Osiris 7, pp. 142-224.

Patzig, G. 1986. "Einleitung" to Frege, Gottlob: *Logische Untersuchungen*, 3rd ed., Göttingen, Vandenhoeck & Ruprecht, pp.5-29.

Peacock, G. 1834. "Report on the Recent Progress and Present State of Certain Branches of Analysis". In *Report of the Third Meeting of the British*

Association for the Advancement of Science held at Cambridge in 1833. London, John Murray, pp. 185-352.

Peckhaus, V. 1994. "Wozu Algebra der Logik? Ernst Schröders Suche nach einer universalen Theorie der Verknüpfungen". Modern Logic 4, pp. 357-381.

Peckhaus, V. 2004. Schröder's Logic. In Gabbay & Woods, pp. 557-609.

Ruffino, M. A. 1991. "Context Principle, Fruitfulness of Logic and the Cognitive Value of Arithmetic in Frege". In *History and Philosophy of Logic* 12, pp. 185-194.

Schröder, E. 1873. *Lehrbuch der Arithmetik und Algebra*. Lepizig, B. G. Teubner.

Schröder, E. 1880. Review of *Begriffsschrift* by Gottlob Frege. In *Zeitschrift für Mathematik und Physik* 25, pp. 81-94.

Schröder, E. 1890. *Vorlesungen über die Algebra der Logik (exacte Logik)*, vol. 1. Leipzig, Teubner.

Schröder, E. 1895. *Vorlesungen über die Algebra der Logik (exacte Logik)*, vol. 3 Part 1: *Algebra und Logik der Relative*. Leipzig, Teubner.

Schröder, E. 1901. (Unsigned) "Grossherzolglich Badischer Hofrat Dr. phil. Ernst Schröder ord. Professor der Mathematik an der Technischen Hochschule i. Baden". In *Geistiges Deutschland. Deutsche Zeitgenossen auf dem Gebiete der Literatur, Wissenschaft und Musik*. Berlin, Adolf Eckstein.

Sullivan, P. M. 2004. "Frege's Logic". In Gabbay & Woods 2004, pp. 659-750..

Trendelenburg, F. A. 1867. "Über Leibnizens Entwurf einer allgemeinen Charakteristik". In *Historische Beiträge zur Philosophie*, vol. 3: *Vermischte Abhandlungen*. Berlín, Bethge, pp. 1-47.

van Heijenoort, J. 1967. "Logic as Calculus And Logic As Language". *Synthese* 24, pp. 324-330. Reprinted in *Selected Essays*. Naples, Bibliopolis, 1985, pp. 11-16.

4

Away from the Facts

Symbolic Knowledge in Husserl's Philosophy of Mathematics[*]

JAIRO JOSÉ DA SILVA

In a letter addressed to Carl Stumpf in the winter of 1890 or 1891[1] Husserl noted that "general arithmetic", which for him included analysis and the theory of functions, finds application to the theories of cardinal and ordinal numbers as well as continuous magnitudes and n-dimensional manifolds in general. In order to account for this variety of applications, Husserl had planned for the second volume of his *Philosophy of Arithmetic* (*PA*, first volume published in 1891) to show that the concept of cardinal number forms the foundation of general arithmetic, and hence that this science has a "content", a ruling concept. But his efforts to carry out his plans were frustrated, and he eventually realized that what he wanted to show could not be shown; as a consequence, the second volume of *PA* never saw the light of day.[2] Now, since "no common concept underlies these applications of arithmetic, from which that science can be derived", i.e., since there is no concept of which general arithmetic constitutes the theoretical investigation, he asks: "what constitutes its content?" In other words, what is general arithmetic a theory of? If arithmetic deals with mere "signs", Husserl considered, if it is a "mere game with symbols" (a view he attributed to Helmholtz), how, he asks, "can a mere game with signs admit of applications?" This question brings to the fore of Husserl's philosophical cogitations at that time the problem of symbolic knowledge, that is, knowledge obtained through the manipulation of symbols, with or without a determinate material content.

---

[*] This paper is dedicated to my beloved Shoshana and Uri, inexhaustible sources of unconditional love.
[1] *Hua* XXI, pp. 244-251, translated in Dallas Willard (ed.) **1994**, pp. 12-19. D. Willard thinks 1891 is the more probable date.
[2] But many preparatory sketches survived (most appear in *Hua* XII, some in *Hua* XXI); some are mentioned and quoted from throughout this paper.

Instead of the planned completion of *PA*, Husserl wrote, and eventually published in 1900-01, his opera magna, *Logical Investigations* (*LI*). In the first part of this book, entitled *Prolegomena to Pure Logic* (completed in 1896, as Husserl himself informed us), he says, concerning the concept of formal manifold (that was by then becoming common currency in mathematics), and the typically mathematical method of extending by purely formal means a formal manifold (or theory) into another (the formal theory of real numbers into the formal theory of complex numbers is the example Husserl gives) that: "In this concept we indeed have the key for the only possible solution of the problem [...]: how impossible (essenceless) concepts can be methodologically treated like real ones" (§70). So, not later than 1896, Husserl had already developed a strategy involving the notion of formal theory to account for imaginary or impossible entities. As we will see later, the solution he presented for the problem of imaginaries in mathematics in the Göttingen conferences of 1901 goes precisely in this direction. Considering that in the *Prolegomena* Husserl also presented a logical-epistemological justification of formal theories *per se* (and that in *PA* he had already successfully justified epistemologically manipulations involving numerical symbols with content) we can safely claim that between 1890-1 and 1896 Husserl found what he took for a satisfactory answer to the epistemological and methodological problem posed by purely symbolic methods in mathematics in all its variants.[3]

But before hitting on the concepts relevant for dealing with the problem of symbolic knowledge (formal mathematics being the exemplary instance), Husserl had to leave the somewhat narrow theoretical frame of *PA*, centered on genetic investigations of a psychological nature on the concept of number together with a logical-epistemological justification of the computational apparatus of arithmetic, for a much broader philosophical perspective from where to approach *ab ovo* the whole set of new logical and epistemological questions the problem of formal mathematics opened up to him. The fact that formal mathematics thrived and had an important role in the acquisition of knowledge (even knowledge about the physical world) could not, for Husserl, be simply a matter of *fact*, it had to be a matter of *right*; and, he thought, it is the task of logic – for logic is the science of science[4] – to

---

[3] Some aspects of which will be further refined latter, in particular the inclusion of the notion of definiteness in the Göttingen talks that I will discuss below.

[4] For Husserl, symbolic knowledge is only knowledge if justified, i.e. if it is proven that it *must* lead to knowledge, despite its lack of intuitive content: "all the artificial operations on signs are in a way at the service of knowledge, but in fact they do not all lead to knowledge in the true and authentic sense of logical comprehension [*Einsicht*]. It is only if the process is itself a logical process, if we have logical comprehension that it must lead to truth, as it is, and because it is so, that its result are not only simply *de facto* true, but the knowledge of truth." *Semiotic* (*Hua* XII, pp. 340-373, 1890), pp. 368-69. It is, in particular, a task for logic to establish the conditions of validity, the extent and the limits of symbolic knowledge: "a truly fecund formal logic is constituted first of all as a logic of signs, which, when sufficiently developed, will form one of the most important parts of logic in general (as the art of

examine, understand, circumscribe, and justify the methods of science. So, the fact that formal mathematics was useful, in mathematics itself and in science, required a *logical* explanation, which, of course, demanded the very map of logic to be redrawn to include new provinces devoted to the investigation of formal domains and formal axiomatic systems (and, most importantly, their interplay).[5] In short, formal mathematics presented for Husserl a problem that required the *Logical Investigations* and subsequent works to be adequately handled (Husserl's precise drawing of the limits of formal logic will appear only in *Formal and Transcendental Logic – FTL*, 1929; English translation-1969). So, I think it is not to overstate to claim that the puzzle posed by symbolic means of knowing, was, during the first half of the last decade of the 19th century, a driving force (if not *the* driving force) in the philosophical developments that led to the phenomenology of *LI* and beyond.

Some analytic philosophers (FØllesdal in particular, in his master's dissertation of 1958), however, came too quickly to the conclusion that it was Frege's (to my view cruelly unfair) review of *PA* (published in 1894) the responsible for Husserl turning the back on the "psychologism" of that earlier work (whose "naivety" Husserl would latter admit), and embark on the project of *LI*. This thesis has been conclusively shown, by Claire Ortiz Hill in particular (see Ortiz Hill **1991**), to not survive a simple analysis of dates. But, surprisingly, virtually no attention has been paid in the literature to the epistemological problem that *did* push Husserl's philosophical career into a new direction, the problem of symbolic knowledge, precisely.[6] One of my goals here is to remedy this situation.

One of the forms the problem of symbolic knowledge takes in Husserl's philosophy is the following: given a domain of objects ruled by a concept (i.e. the domain constitutes the extension of the concept), in what circumstances are we allowed to extend this domain by adding to it purely formal objects (objects that do not fall under the concept governing the

---

knowledge). The task of logic is here the same as anywhere: to become master of the natural procedures of the spirit that judges, to examine them, to understand the value they have for knowledge in order to assess with exactitude their limits, extent and range, and establish general rules concerning all this." *Semiotic*, p. 373.

[5] Husserl would eventually allocate the highest stratum of apophantic logic (the logic of statements and theories) to the investigation of formal theories, and the highest stratum of formal ontology (the logic of objects considered in the most general sense as "anything whatsoever") to the study of formal domains. About Husserl's conception of logic see da Silva **2000b**.

[6] None of the articles of Seebohm, FØllesdal and Mohanty **1991**, for instance, deals with this question. Although, as I will show below, the problem of symbolic knowledge had already surfaced in *PA* in the form of a quest for epistemological justification for the algorithmic apparatus of arithmetic, Husserl was able to adequately handle this variant of the problem within the theoretical frame of that book (since in this case symbols are meaningful, they denote something). The problem appears in full strength only when *meaningless* symbols are involved.

domain and are only formally characterized) so as to better deal with problems involving only the original objects? The extension of the domain of numbers proper (real numbers) by the adjunction of so-called complex numbers for a better treatment of *real* algebraic equations is a classical example of the benefices of extending a conceptual domain by the adjunction of convenient formal objects. This is what Husserl called the problem of imaginaries in mathematics.

The solution he presented for this problem, the conditions under which "imaginaries" can be allowed in mathematics, have been discussed by many Husserlian scholars (in particular, Majer, Ortiz Hill and myself),[7] but a more encompassing study of the many forms the problem of symbolic knowledge takes in Husserl's philosophy, from the justification of arithmetical computational technology (in *PA*, Husserl's first philosophical work) to how to overcome the "symbolic alienation" of modern science (in *The Crisis of European Science and Transcendental Phenomenology*, Husserl's last) and, more importantly, an assessment of the *correctness* of Husserl's "solution" to the problem of imaginaries in mathematics and symbolic knowledge in general is missing in the literature. Another of my aims here is to contribute to fill this gap.

It is possible to extract from Husserl's writings *three* distinct, but not independent answers to the question posed by symbolic knowledge. The *locus classicus* of the first is *PA*; the second, a couple of lectures he presented in 1901, invited by Hilbert, at the Mathematical Society of Göttingen, to which university he had then just moved;[8] and the third, the *Logical Investigations*. For the sake of clarity, I will consider them separately, but bear in mind that they are only different aspects of a single general problem admitting different specifications. In fact, more than three answers, Husserl had three problems, three different questions related to the general problem of symbolic knowledge; each requiring a different treatment, and hence a different answer. I want here to trace a faithful picture of how these "answers" relate to each other and argue for the following conclusions: 1) Husserl was, already in 1890, acutely aware of the problem symbolic knowledge involving meaningless symbols posed for the methodology of *PA*, and hence already moving out of that theoretical perspective; 2) the problem of symbolic knowledge played an essential role in the philosophical developments that led from *PA* to *LI* and beyond; 3) by 1890-91 Husserl had already found the answer to the problem posed by knowledge provided by rule-based manipulations of meaningful symbols,

---

[7] See, for instance, Ortiz Hill **1995**, Majer **1997** and da Silva **2000a** and **2000c**. These authors, however, concentrate mostly on the notion of completeness Husserl introduced as a key player in his treatment of the problem of imaginaries in mathematics.
[8] But the Göttingen lectures are not where it first appears; Husserl had already argued along similar lines with respect to the problem posed by the empty class in Schroeder's calculus of logic (*Review of Schroeder's 'Lessons on the Algebra of Logic'*, in *Hua* XXII, pp. 3-43, translated in D. Willard (ed.) **1994**, pp. 52-91).

and drawn the main line of his approach to the problem concerning the role meaningless symbols can play, and under which conditions, in the context of contentual theories, which would be completely articulated in terms of the notion of logical definiteness (completeness) in the Göttingen lectures of 1901; 4) Husserl found his answer to the problem concerning knowledge provided by formal theories considered in themselves not later than 1896; 5) Husserl did not change his mind about how to account for symbolic knowledge in all its variants for the rest of his life (the solution he presented for the "formalist alienation" of modern physical science in his last work, *The Crisis of European Science and Transcendental Phenomenology*, published in 1954, rests on previous ideas concerning the role symbolic manipulations can play in the acquisition of knowledge *about some specific domain*, the empirical world in this case).

I. Symbolic knowledge involving symbols with *content* (i.e. symbols with a determinate reference): the surrogating role of symbols

A main concern of Husserl's in *PA* is the psychological genesis of arithmetical notions.[9] In it, Husserl showed how we become aware of numbers, i.e., how they are *presented* to consciousness, and how we operate intuitively with them. The problem is that our natural limitations of attention and power of discrimination prevent us from becoming aware of numbers that exceed a certain threshold (which Husserl set around 12) and thus operating intuitively with them. The question then is how to deal with numbers that are not intuitively accessible. This is where symbols come in. It is important to notice that, in this case, symbols have content, *they are not meaningless signs*.

We know there is an infinite sequence of whole numbers, one succeeding the other (with the exclusion, of course, of the first, which succeeds none) in a discrete linear array going on forever, but we cannot intuitively distinguish

---

[9] But we must be careful not to tag his approach as psychologism pure and crude (as Frege did). A problem that accompanied Husserl throughout his philosophical life was how to bridge the gap between the objective "world" (which includes the world of mathematics) and subjectivity. To investigate how we become conscious of mathematical notions, that is, their "genesis", is part of the task. But a "genetic" investigation is not an inquiry on how arithmetic notions come into being, but how they become objects of consciousness. We may very well read *PA* under the assumption that the domain of numbers is an objective domain of independently existing entities. It does not really matter, for Husserl is only concerned with how they become objects *for a subject*. In later works he will explicitly eliminate the possibility of considering objects and subjectivity as independent instances. In his transcendental phenomenological period (from the publication of *Ideas I* on, but already prefigured in previous works) for Husserl, a subject, to the extent that it is a *conscious* subject, is always conscious *of* objects; objects, on the other hand, are always objects *for* a subject. The world, any world, is, as a result of transcendental reduction, simply an intentional correlate of consciousness.

one from the other after a stage in this sequence (which, however, cannot be pinpointed). Nor can we, without counting, attach a number to a given collection of arbitrary objects, if this collection exceeds a certain quantity. But counting is nothing more than representing a given quantity in a symbolic system, the decimal system of notation, the system of numerical words, or any other. This is how it works (in the decimal system): we proceed by grouping the units of a given collection in groups of ten units; then we group these groups in groups of ten, the hundreds; the groups of hundreds in groups of ten, the thousands; and so on. If we get in this process, for instance, seven groups of thousands, three groups oh hundreds, five groups of ten units and six remaining ungrouped units we have counted seven thousand, three hundred and fifty-six: 7,356 in decimal notation.

Analogously, to represent a number symbolically in the decimal system (we can choose any other) is to represent the grouping of its units (a number is, for Husserl, what the tradition since Plato says it is, a collection of undifferentiated units – monads), i.e., to render explicit what the iterative process of grouping in groups of tens, beginning with the units, produces. If we cannot apprehend the units of a number (which we know exists "out there") with clarity, we can at least represent clearly the iterate process of grouping them. To be given this representation is almost as good – if not better, given our limitations – as to be given the number intuitively as a collection of monads that we cannot keep clearly separated in consciousness, if the number exceeds a certain limit. Representing numbers in decimal notation (or any other notational system) *is a way of grasping them and indirectly dealing with them.*

This is how Husserl saw things:[10] we are able to *simultaneously* produce numerical concepts and, by means of notational systems – which are, of course, symbolic systems –, represent symbolically the numbers they characterize *in such a way that the numbers and their symbolic representations stand in an isomorphic correspondence*. In fact, the conceiving of a *specific* number – that is, the production of its concept – generates the symbolic representation of this number in a systematic way. For instance, the *concept* "number containing seven groups of thousands, three groups of hundreds, five groups of tens and six isolated monads" generates immediately the numeral 7,356; any particular numerical concept leads immediately to the symbolic representation of its number. The symbol is generated by the concept; to give the numerical concept is tantamount to giving the symbolic representation of the number it characterizes.[11] Consequently, the domain of numbers and operations among them and the domain of numerals (their symbolic representation in the decimal system)

---

[10] All these ideas, if not always the same words, are scattered throughout the second part of *PA* (although, the word "isomorphism", for instance, is not used, the concept is unmistakably there).

[11] There are, of course, many other ways of producing numerical concepts in mathematics, all leading to some sort of symbolic representation, although not necessarily or immediately the decimal representation.

and symbolic operations (our usual algorithms for operating with these numerals) are the isomorphic image of each other. We *form* numerical concepts simultaneously with the symbolic representations of the numbers they denote, and can *only* operate with these numbers by operating symbolically with their representations. Since the domain of numbers and that of symbols are isomorphic, by manipulating symbols correctly we can produce correct numerical results.[12]

We can easily conceive a process of generating numbers indefinitely; we can even conceive them all as independently existing entities, but we can only have a grasp on them symbolically. If grasping a number in its individuality counts as intuiting it, then symbolization is the only way of *intuiting* large numbers, contradictory as it may seem. But if we think, as Husserl did, that to intuit a number *properly* is to contemplate all of its monads *clearly* and *distinctively simultaneously*, then we do not have any proper intuition of large numbers. But, with the help of symbolization we have the next best thing, which may very well count as a form of semi-intuition. Numerical symbols are then, from this perspective, mere surrogates of numbers, but *essential* ones; they allow us to grasp and manipulate what we cannot reach *in any other way*.[13] By dealing *intuitively* (in a form of intuition close to and based on sense perception) with numerical symbols we deal, semi-intuitively or indirectly, if you want, with numbers proper. And this is possible because the object of knowledge (the domain of numbers and its operations) and its symbolic representation (the system of numerals and algorithmic rules) are *formally indistinguishable*.

In "Semiotic" Husserl considered also the problem of logically justifying symbolic *reasoning* in general, not only symbolic arithmetical *computations*, as in *PA*. Inquiring on the logical and psychological processes involved in successful symbolic reasoning – that is, one that effectively produces knowledge –, he says that, in order to be a logically sound process, symbolic reasoning must fulfill two conditions: 1) "the systematic forms of junction of words [*symbolic expressions*, *JJS*] must reflect exactly those of thinking [*meaningful judgments*, *JJS*], otherwise the former could never become habitual substitutes for the latter" and 2) "the first part of the system, which contains the premises [...], must manifestly determine in a purely formal manner, univocally, the part that contains the conclusion [...] the set of premises determine univocally the conclusion". So, for Husserl, the soundness of symbolic reasoning depends on the fulfillment of two requirements. The first asks for *exact* correspondence between judgments and symbolic expressions, that is, syntactically well-formed symbolic expressions must express meaningful judgments, and conversely, meaningful

---

[12] The possibility (which worried Leibniz) that symbolic reasoning can induce errors is in this way completely eliminated.

[13] So, for Husserl, the use of symbols is much more than a mere auxiliary devise for thinking, which we resort to in order to basically help our memory; according to him, symbols make our psychic life, including thinking itself, *possible* (see *Semiotic*, p. 349).

judgments must always be able to be expressed symbolically by a syntactically correct expression (so, in this case too, symbolic expressions have content); the second, that our conclusions (i.e. our stock of true judgments) must be derived in a purely mechanical and symbolic manner from the premises. The symbolic as a "mirror image" and surrogate of the intuitive or contentual that is at the basis of Husserl's logical justification of symbolic *calculations* with meaningful numerical symbols (i.e., symbols with content) is also required of symbolic *derivations* involving contentual symbolic "judgments".

Another interesting quote comes from another text of 1891[14]: "any algorithm first establishes a rigorous parallel correspondence between fundamental concepts, fundamental judgments and fundamental chains of reasoning and algorithmic elements. In fact, the objects of the domain, which are represented in an indeterminate manner, are replaced by simple signs; composites of objects, by composites of signs, established by means of signs of operation that correspond to the different concepts of operation; the relations, by signs of relation. Moreover, the fundamental propositions [are replaced] by symbolic conventions telling which are the permitted symbolic modifications (to the extent that they correspond to true judgments) and which are not. Concomitantly, conventional meanings are given to the symbols; hence, algorithmic concepts are one-to-one coordinated with the original concepts." (p.418). Again, logically justified symbolic systems must "mimic" the domain of knowledge they stand for, and, like systems of calculations with meaningful symbols vis-à-vis their interpretations, act as a surrogate for it.[15]

This first treatment of the problem of symbolic knowledge is still very limited (since it only takes into consideration *interpreted* symbolisms), as Husserl inevitably recognized when he had to consider more general arithmetic systems, as we will see next. Although there is one thing Husserl certainly noticed, that the manipulation of symbols can produce knowledge only if the symbolic system *represents* somehow the system of objects we aim to know, there is something I am not absolutely sure he realized (for he does not mention it explicitly), that a *possible* basis for a relation of representation between two systems is structural identity (in which case both systems instantiate exactly *the same abstract structure*). We can investigate one by examining the other because the object of our investigation is presented indifferently in either one. Symbolic knowledge is only knowledge

---

[14] *Hua* XII, pp 408-29: "On the Concept of Operation".

[15] "[...] the proper task of a calculus is to be, for an entire domain of knowledge, a method of symbolic deduction of consequences; hence, an art for substituting, by means of an appropriate designation of ideas, a calculus for effective deductions; that is, a conversion and a substitution according to rules of signs by signs and then, by virtue of the correspondence between signs and ideas, for obtaining from the final formulas the desired judgments." (*Hua* XII, p. 259)

of that which is at the basis of the relation of representation, namely, a common abstract formal structure.

II. Imaginary elements in mathematics, symbolic knowledge involving *meaningless* signs: the psycho-technical role of symbols[16]

Husserl never doubted the value of meaningless formalism for knowledge[17]. The problem of how to account for meaningless symbols being successfully treated, for methodological purposes, as if denoting something had already surfaced in *PA*. Since 0 and 1 do not denote numbers, for "nothing" and "one" are not answers to the question "how many?", Husserl could only justify their *necessary* inclusion in arithmetic on purely *practical* grounds. According to him, "we would be quickly led into embarrassing complications and even serious inconveniences in the theory of numbers if we wanted to keep 0 and 1 apart from numbers proper and renounce to give these two kinds a common denomination" (*PA*, *Hua* XII, p. 145). And "if we consider that a uniform operational activity according to rules is not possible unless all imaginable results of an operation can be treated formally in the same way, it becomes clear why this enlargement of the domain of calculation was indeed an important progress towards the establishment of arithmetic" (ibid. pp. 146-7). The same problem also appeared, regarding the empty class, in Schroeder's calculus of logic. Schroeder defined the empty class as that which is contained in any other class, a definition Husserl considered absurd for, he thought, there are non-overlapping classes. For Husserl, the use of meaningless symbols in contentual theories, such as the empty class in Schroeder's calculus, or the imaginary unit in arithmetic, could be pragmatically justified only if these symbols were in principle dispensable.[18] This is essentially the answer he gives to this variant of the problem of symbolic knowledge, when meaningless symbols and their

---

[16] Concerning details of Husserl's vindication of imaginaries in mathematics, as presented in the Göttingen lectures, I refer the reader to my previous papers da Silva **2000a** and **2000c**.

[17] "The solution of problems raised within a theoretical discipline, or one of its theories, can at times derive the most effective methodological help from recourse to the categorial type or (what is the same) to the form of the theory, and perhaps also by going over to a more comprehensive form or class of forms and to its laws." (*LU*, Prolegomena to Pure Logic, § 70)

[18] "[T]his 'creative' definition of 0 does not give it yet the right to exist in the system of the calculus [...] – however, is there anything that can give it such a right? Of such a thing I cannot find the shadow of a proof. The 0 of the calculus of identity presents the same problem of $\sqrt{-1}$ in the arithmetical calculus. In one as in the other case, we can only give the correspondent proof by considering the corresponding algorithmic technique. Here, it would be necessary to show that any relation deduced with the help of 0, which involves moreover only symbols that are real [*i.e. meaningful* – *JJS*], must be a valid relation according exclusively to the meaning of these symbols and the laws that concern them. Creative definitions do not contribute with anything, even if they preserve the internal consistency of the calculus. The question is not whether the calculus remains consistent, but whether it remains a calculus of classes." (*Review of Schroeder*, p. 269)

formal properties are allowed to interfere with contentual theories; one to which he will always adhere. The problem of "imaginaries" in mathematics will be better articulated, however, in the so-called Göttingen lectures.[19]

In 1901 Husserl moved to Göttingen, coming from Halle. In the same year, Hilbert, a shining star in the Gottingen mathematical community, invited him to give a talk in the local mathematical society. Husserl chosen subject for what turned out to be two talks was the imaginary in mathematics, which he understood as including not only complex, but also negative, irrational and even rational numbers; in short, any number that was not "natural", i.e. a non-negative integer answering the question "how many?". Obviously, this choice was not accidental; Husserl was in fact dialoguing with Hilbert, whose axiomatization of geometry and the theory of real numbers involved some ideas and concepts Husserl considered relevant to *his* answer to the problem of imaginaries, but whose approach to the question of ideal elements in mathematics (which would some years later become more articulated in the so-called formalist program for the foundations of mathematics) did not satisfy him.

This problem, as Husserl understood it, was the following: consider an axiomatic system designed to describe a given well-determined mathematical domain, such as, for instance, the integers. This is, of course, an *interpreted* system. Suppose now that we introduce operations in this domain *explicitly contradicting* axiomatic principles; for instance, the square rooting of negative numbers – thus introducing *complex* numbers in the original domain. To what extent are we justified in using these new entities to prove *anything whatsoever* concerning the elements of the original domain? Analogously if we introduced new members in a given domain simply by stipulation, extending to them, in a purely formal manner, the operations that were originally defined (and meaningful) *only* for the elements of the narrower domain.

In 1899 Hilbert had published his *Foundations of Geometry* in which he presented the first complete axiomatization of Euclidian geometry and proved its consistency relative to arithmetic. In 1900 he had also presented an axiomatization of the theory of the real numbers. In the former work Hilbert explicitly considered axiomatic geometry as a *non-interpreted* symbolic system admitting any interpretation that satisfied the axioms (Hilbert's famous tables, chairs and beer mugs for points, lines and planes). This removal of content was a pre-condition for the metamathematical work to be done, for it allowed a proof of the consistency of geometry relative to arithmetic by explicitly exhibiting arithmetical models of geometrical systems. Later, when Hilbert conceived his program of foundation of

---

[19] We have in fact only Husserl's notes for the talks, not a text meant for publication. This, of course, poses many great difficulties for the reader (see da Silva **2000a** for a detailed discussion of the content of these notes as far as the problem of imaginaries in mathematics is concerned).

mathematics by means of axiomatization plus proofs of *absolute* consistency by finitary means, taking axiomatic systems as purely formal symbolic systems remained an essential methodological strategy.

In his paper "The Concept of Number" of 1900, the axiomatic method substituted the so-called genetic treatments of the concept of real number (like, for instance, those of Cantor and Dedekind), in which real numbers are *defined* in terms of other number concepts by means of set theoretical constructions. Hilbert's idea was to characterize the domain of real numbers axiomatically as the *only* domain (up to isomorphism) satisfying a certain collection of axioms (in modern terms, to characterize it by a *categorical* system of axioms). To accomplish the task Hilbert had to add to some familiar looking axioms referring directly to numbers an extra axiom – which he called axiom of completeness – of a completely different character. Its task was to select among many possible models for the remaining axioms that which could not be further enlarged by the adjunction of new elements, i.e. the model that was complete in an *ontological* sense. (But Hilbert was not totally satisfied with this axiom; its peculiar metamathematical and purely *ad hoc* character did not appeal to him very much. It was eventually substituted by a more strictly mathematical axiom in later axiomatizations of the theory).

Two basic ideas in Hilbert's works are also central in Husserl's treatment of the problem of imaginaries: the notion of a non-interpreted axiomatic system and the concept of completeness. Both agreed on what the former was, but Husserl's concept of completeness differed essentially from Hilbert's; whereas for Hilbert completeness was an ontological notion, for Husserl it was eminently *logical*. In strict analogy with modern notions of completeness, for Husserl, *theories*, not *domains*, were complete.[20]

---

[20] I say Hilbert's axiom of completeness has an *ontological* sense because it is designed to select, up to isomorphism, a particular *domain of objects* (unlike the *meta-logical* notion of completeness, which applies to axiomatic *systems* and describes the property of the system of being able to decide, in a syntactic or semantic sense, everything that can be stated in its language). In the axiomatization of arithmetic the task of Hilbert's axiom is to select the ordered field of *real numbers* among other ordered fields. This axiom appears also in the axiomatization of geometry: it is impossible to extend a *set of points on a line*, with its order and congruence relations, so as to preserve the relations existing among the original elements as well as the fundamental properties of line order and congruence that follow from the other axioms (Hilbert **1971**). Husserl's notion of definiteness, on the other hand, as introduced in the Göttingen talks, was clearly designed to express the *deductive* notion of completeness. It may be the case that Husserl *thought* (erroneously) that this, like Hilbert completeness, would guarantee the *categoricity* of the system, and then the circumscription of an *intended* model (up to isomorphism); but obviously categoricity was not *explicitly* intended in Husserl's characterization of definiteness for axiomatic systems. Contrasting Hilbert's and deductive notions of completeness, A. Fraenkel says that "in the latter [i.e. Hilbert's notion of completeness appearing in the axiomatization of geometry and the arithmetic of the real numbers - *JJS*] it is the objects governed by the axioms, in the former [i.e. deductive or Husserl's notion of completeness - *JJS*] the axioms themselves that are not capable of extension." (A. Fraenkel, *Einleitung in die Mengenlehre*, 3^d ed., Berlin: Springer, 1928, p. 347)

There is still another notion, that of *consistency*, whose central position in Hilbert's theory of real numbers – and in his later "program" – is beyond dispute, but which Husserl displaced, in his solution of the problem of imaginaries, from the *isolated* central position in which Hilbert had put it. For Hilbert the centrality of this notion was unquestionable: since the domain of real numbers had to be *exclusively* characterized – or defined – by the system of axioms, in order for there to be such a domain it was necessary (and, for Hilbert, also sufficient) that the axiomatic system were *consistent*, i.e. that no contradiction could be derived from the axioms. Hilbert considered the task of showing that the axiomatic theory of real numbers was consistent so important that he put it second in his list of guiding problems for the new century in his famous address to the International Congress of Mathematicians of 1900.

Husserl obviously knew of all this, but he did not agree completely with Hilbert. As we will see, Husserl thought that only *his* notion of completeness allowed for a satisfactory answer of the problem of imaginaries. It is clear that Husserl chose to speak about this problem in Göttingen in order to have the chance of offering some criticism of Hilbert's approach to the theory of real numbers – and, by extension, similar solutions of the problem of imaginaries in mathematics – which he saw as *epistemologically* flawed.

This is how Husserl saw the matter:

The basic fact is that we cannot introduce operations in a domain that are explicitly forbidden by the concept governing this domain. Then the only way of so doing or, equivalently, enlarging a given domain is by divesting its theory of any interpretation. This is what Husserl called *abstracting* the *form* out of an interpreted axiomatic theory in order to transform it into a *form of theory*, or still, a *formal theory*; this was accomplished by simply refusing to give the terms of the theory a definite domain and its operations a definite meaning. All the symbols became mere signs. It was now possible to enlarge this non-interpreted theory by the introduction, via definitions, of *new* signs denoting *new* purely formal elements and operations.

Of course, this extension had to be consistent, if we wanted this system to have any interpretation at all. For Hilbert this would be enough, for it would guarantee that we could not derive in the larger system a sentence whose negation were a theorem of the narrower system, for this would immediately introduce an inconsistency in the larger system (since it *extended* the narrower system). But this solution of the problem of imaginaries (imaginary elements are acceptable provided they do not introduce inconsistencies) is not acceptable for Husserl. His criticism is analogous to that which the intuitionists offered to Hilbert's suggestion of identifying freedom from contradiction with existence (but the resemblance is circumstantial; Husserl was never an intuitionist in the sense this word has in the philosophy of mathematics). According to Husserl, the fact that we could derive in the larger system a sentence *involving only the symbols of the narrower system*, which was, moreover, consistent with anything derivable in this narrower system, does not mean that this sentence is *true* of the elements of the domain the narrower system was designed to describe in the first place (before formal abstraction). Consistency does not equal truth (as, by the way, Kant had already stressed).

For Husserl, formal abstraction was instrumental in avoiding absurdness in extending interpreted axiomatic systems, but in the end these system were always though as describing definite, conceptually circumscribed domains of objects. A system describing the natural numbers, for example, could be divested of interpretation in order to be extend into a (consistent) system that could be interpreted by, say, the real numbers; but *no sentence* of the original system that was provable in this larger system could be accepted as a *true* assertion about *natural numbers* if it were not provable in the original system. As Husserl puts it, a system must be *the master of its domain*. But when this happens? According to him, when the system is *definite*, that is, *logically* complete: any sentence of this system, that is, any sentence that can be written exclusively with the symbols of the system, must be *decided in it*, i.e. the sentence or its negation (but not both) must be provable *in the system*. No enlargement should be required to do the work the system was designed to do; a system can, of course, be divested of interpretation and extended – with the addition of *new* symbols – to a system that can be interpreted as a theory of a larger domain of objects, but this larger system cannot help the original one do the work it was supposed to do *by itself*. The idea of a definite system of axioms, a *nomological system* as Husserl also called it, answers to the Aristotelian ideal of science that Husserl was not willing to abandon. More importantly, such a requirement was indispensable if we were to equate, as, according to Husserl, the idea of a *theoretical* science demanded, true-in-a-domain with derivable-in-the-theory-of-the-domain.

What is then, from the perspective of Husserl's criticism of Hilbert in the Göttingen talks, the role of imaginaries in mathematics; how can they be vindicated? The answer is simple and straightforward: imaginary elements can be useful in deriving truths referring to domains where they have no interpretation (which would maybe be more difficult to derive without their help) but, in the end, they must be completely dispensable, since these truths must, in principle, be obtainable without their intervention. The manipulation of symbols that do *not* correspond to anything in the domain of an interpreted theory can produce knowledge in this domain *only if* this knowledge can in principle be obtained within the limits of the theory in question. According to Husserl, *meaningless symbols cannot be essential to knowledge*, at least as far as the knowledge of *conceptually determined* objectual domains is concerned.

At first sight, it may seem strange that Husserl presented this solution for the problem of imaginaries *after* developing the views of the *Logical Investigations*, where he presented a whole satisfactory logical-epistemological vindicating of *purely* symbolic logical systems *per se*. In order to understand this apparent contradiction we must notice that the problem Husserl was addressing in the Göttingen lectures was *not* the epistemological justification of formal mathematics in and for itself, but the logical justification of *using* formal mathematics for solving problems in *contentual* mathematics. We can read the treatment he presented in Göttingen as an answer to a more restricted problem – not how to make sense of imaginaries, but how to justify their *intromission* into *other* numerical domains in which they have no meaning. From this perspective, there is no contradiction between the approach to imaginaries in the Göttingen lectures and other strategies of justification for symbolic knowledge in *LI*.

III. Symbolic knowledge as formal ontology (symbolic *knowledge proper*): the structural role of symbols

Frustrated efforts to write the second volume of *PA* gradually pulled Husserl away from the *genetic* approach he favored for the treatment of the natural numbers.[21] He eventually came to believe that an *axiomatic* approach to what he called "general arithmetic", that is, the arithmetic of other number concepts, such as the integers, both positive and negative, or the real and the complex numbers was more appropriated. Even *before* the publication of *PA* Husserl was aware of the possibilities of axiomatic systems as ways of mastering, by symbolic means, arbitrary domains of entities.

In a paper on set theory of 1891,[22] for instance, Husserl developed the arithmetic of positive integers, i.e. numbers that correspond to the concept of quantity, as an *interpreted* axiomatic theory, and in a paper on the concept of general arithmetic of 1890[23] he suggested that *non-interpreted* axiomatic systems were the best (maybe only) way of dealing with more general concepts of number.

It is not difficult to see why he thought so. He believed that any *a priori* contentual axiomatic theory was necessarily a conceptual theory, that is, the theory of a concept under which the objects of the relevant domain were assembled.[24] The theory of a concept being nothing more than the development of the logical consequences of a few explicative, intuitively clear axioms (founded on some form of conceptual intuition). The problem is that, unlike the natural numbers, general numerical concepts (negative, irrational...) are exclusively determined by their operational properties: the negative number $-n$ is the number that added to n results in 0; an irrational

---

[21] In *PA*, not only our awareness of numbers is explained in terms of a (psychological) mechanism of genesis; numerical concepts, together with their symbolic representations, also make their appearance in a systematic process of generation.
[22] *Hua* XII, pp. 385-407: "On Set Theory".
[23] *Hua* XII, pp. 375-379: "The Concept of General Arithmetic".
[24] See *Hua* XII, pp. 380-84: "Arithmetic as an A Priori Science". No date is given in *Hua*; the date given in J. English's translation to French is 1891.

number is only the limit of a sequence of rational numbers; the complex number *i* is (stipulated as) that number whose square equals -1.

Whereas the natural numbers can be conceived as sets of undifferentiated units upon which we can operate, adding or removing some, thus generating all numbers, the operations on negative, irrational or complex numbers are defined only formally. Whereas the theory of the natural numbers can be built on an axiomatic explanation of the process of generating numbers, the only way of giving the other number concepts a theory is by raising their defining formal properties to the status of axioms; symbols for operations denoting only operations on symbols, and numerical terms only the idea of entities upon which operations can be performed. In short, the axiomatic theories of general number concepts must be *purely formal* theories.

This raises some questions: in what sense a purely formal theory *represents* all its models (which, incidentally, are in general non-isomorphic)? What is a purely formal theory the theory of? How to vindicate purely formal theories epistemologically? The answer to these questions will emerge clearly in *LI* and some subsequent works and will constitute Husserl's way of vindicating epistemologically non-interpreted (formal) theories *per se*.

A purely formal theory, as Husserl saw things then, describes a purely formal realm of being (a formal manifold), a *form* different interpretations of the theory will substantiate with different matter. By symbolic manipulations within this system we are indirectly dealing with all its interpretations or models, *but exclusively with respect to their (common) form* (or *structure*).

Consider a *non-interpreted* theory, which we can think of merely as a calculus, i.e. a rule-abiding game with symbols and symbolic configurations, like chess. Provided this theory is formally consistent it can be seen as the theory *of* an objectively given *intentional* domain, thus making a symbolic "game" into knowledge of something, a specific domain, which however is pure form and no content – a structural skeleton underlying all the materially determinate interpretations of the theory. If this theory has many different non-isomorphic interpretations, we know them all, but only formally, since a formal skeleton is all they have in common. It is as if by playing with symbols we investigate many different, not necessarily isomorphic domains *simultaneously*, but only as far as the calculus can reach, that is, their formal structure, which *only* can be symbolically represented.

Symbolic knowledge has to do *exclusively* with how objects relate with each other regardless of their particular nature or the particular nature of the operations and relations involved, that is, with the formal properties of mathematical manifolds of a certain type; it tells nothing about the *specific nature* of the objects inhabiting these manifolds. A non-interpreted theory describes *empty* formal structures irrespectively of their eventual material fillings. In *LI*, Husserl clearly realized (stating it explicitly) that a non-interpreted, purely symbolic theory is *nothing but* the theory of the empty *form* of materially determinate objectual domains, and that such a theory, more than just a game with symbols, gives us *formal knowledge*, i.e. knowledge of objective forms (of actual or merely possible domains). Symbolic knowledge provides us with knowledge of not necessarily actually existing, but in general only merely possible objectual domains, but only with respect to their forms. In short, symbolic knowledge belongs to what Husserl called *formal ontology*.

By denoting an object *generically considered* by an object-symbol (a nominal term), an operation of a certain type *generically considered* by an operation-symbol, a relation of a certain type *generically considered* by a relation-symbol we create a language in which to describe a *formal domain*, that is, the empty form of possibly existing objectual domains of a certain type; by *presupposing* certain formal properties in this domain – which we can express by means of symbolic expressions of the appropriate language (for instance, the symbolic identity expressing the commutativity of an indeterminate binary operation denoted by an operation-symbol) – we put together a theory of the domain, which Husserl thought merely as the form of possibly existing conceptual theories (if the formal theory is consistent); to develop this theory by means of formal logic (which, as we know, is content independent and context free) is part of what Husserl called formal ontology in *Ideas I* (1913) and *Formal and Transcendental Logic* (1929). In short, symbolic knowledge gives us knowledge of forms of actual or only logically possible objectual domains, and the goal of formal ontology is the exhaustive investigation of such forms, in themselves and their mutual correlations.

In *LI* (particularly §§ 69-71 of *Prolegomena to Pure Logic*), Husserl presented the idea of a pure science of logical forms and, correlatively, forms of theories, as a necessary completion of the ideal of a pure theory of science or, simply, pure logic. Husserl was then clearly influenced by the creation of what he called *formal mathematics* by mathematicians such as Grassmann, Hamilton, Lie and Cantor, who in different ways and for different purposes developed (formal) theories of formal manifolds, such as n-dimensional Euclidian and non-Euclidian spaces, transformations groups and unstructured sets, and studied their formal properties. Husserl saw formal mathematics as a *science*, not a meaningless play with symbols, to be included however in the realm of pure logic, whose task was to give us *a priori* knowledge of the formal aspects of no matter which objectual domains we may happen to stumble on. For Husserl, formal mathematics was justifiable as a sort of pre-occupation (in a literal sense).

Concluding Remarks

Let us sum up and summarize. By the time Husserl published *PA* (1891) he was already deeply involved with the task of providing sound *logical* (that is, *epistemological*) foundations for general arithmetic (since this was the main goal of a planned but never published sequel to *PA*). He had by then already left behind most of the theoretical framework of his first book (actually a rewritten version of his dissertation of 1887), in particular the project of grounding more general concepts of number in the notion of cardinal number. In 1891, it was already clear to Husserl that he could not treat negative, irrational or complex numbers as somehow "growing out" of non-negative integers (for one, these numbers do not correspond to a notion of quantity).

But, unlike Kant, Husserl was not willing to let them go; he accepted unreservedly the *validity*, already well established in mathematics, of the use of these general concepts of number. But, on the other hand, he did not see how familiar mathematical methods involving generalized notions of number could be justified on the basis of the understanding of fundamental concepts, such as number and quantity (on the basis of which remember the methods of the arithmetic of finite cardinal numbers were justified). These methods could not, in particular, like the symbolic methods of cardinal arithmetic, be proven to be sound on the basis of a notion of representation, since general arithmetic is not conceptually founded and negative, irrational or complex numbers, Husserl thinks, do not stand for anything. He then took upon himself the task of finding a justification for the purely symbolic general concepts of number and the mathematical methods based on them.[25] This, Husserl believed, was a task for *formal logic*.[26] It was the beginning of the road leading to his *Logical Investigations*.

As is evident in *Semiotic*, Husserl had already realized as early as 1890 that the justification of the validity of the methods of general arithmetic should rest on the distinction between *material content* and materially empty *form*, both for judgments and theories, and that the contribution general arithmetic brings to mathematical knowledge has to do with the knowledge of forms (formal knowledge).[27] Husserl viewed general arithmetic as a *symbolic calculus*, to be logically justified as such: general arithmetic, he says, "aims to establish a system of rules that renders possible a process of

---

[25] It is never idle to emphasize that the necessary reference of knowledge to evidence – a thesis already present in *PA*, but that is even more central in Husserl's later philosophy – does not necessarily imply the non-validity of symbolic methods. It only imposes on the formal logician the task of justifying them as logically (epistemologically) sound. We must be *sure* that symbolic reasoning yields knowledge, and it is the logician's task to show that it indeed does.

[26] "Every calculation, for example, an addition, is a symbolic formation of truth by means of certain operations on fundamental signs. All the artificial operations on signs serve, in a certain way, the goals of knowledge, but they do not lead in fact to knowledge in the true and authentic sense of logical comprehension [*Einsichten*]. It is only if the process itself is a logical process, if we have the logical comprehension that it must lead to truth, as it is, and because it is such, that its results will not be simply *de facto* true, but the knowledge of truth." *Semiotic*, pp. 368-9.

[27] "The best proof that the separation we have established between matter and form has effectively a value for formal logic is provided by the sciences in which a truly vast and fecund reasoning takes place by means of formal mechanisms: the sciences of numbers, magnitudes and extensions." (*Semiotic*, 349-50)

mechanical calculation [my emphasis]".[28] Immediately after this quote, however, Husserl criticizes the traditional way of seeing general arithmetic as a "calculus with letters". He thinks there is no justification for this, and claims that we can still consider general arithmetic as a calculus with numbers, *provided we divested the signs of operations and relations among numerical terms of their usual meanings*. Briefly, general arithmetic is a *purely symbolic* system, but it cannot be justified as a mere calculus with letters, for such a calculus cannot have anything to do with knowledge. It is a task for the formal logician to find out under which conditions a purely symbolic system can be epistemologically relevant.

But could not general arithmetic, although not a conceptual theory, be all the same contentual? Not for Husserl, empirical theories can possibly be non-conceptual and contentual, but not *a priori* theories. In a text of 1891,[29] inquiring on the nature of arithmetic as an *a priori* science, Husserl says that, by nature, such a theory "does not begin with single facts for then to obtain possibly true generalities by induction, but immediately by certain generalities that are apodictically certain and immediately evident, which one acquires by simply presenting to oneself certain 'fundamental concepts' that produces, by means of mediate evidence and certitude, the entire sequence of theorems." That is, *a priori contentual* sciences are *conceptual* sciences, the intuition of whose fundamental concepts provides all their fundamental axiomatic truths; all the rest follow by logic. Along these lines Husserl carried out (in another paper of the same year[30]) a treatment of arithmetic based on set theory, since, he believed, the concept of cardinality is the founding concept of the arithmetic of cardinal numbers. But, although a priori and axiomatic, general arithmetic is not a conceptual science. There was no other option for Husserl than to take its axioms, and the axioms of any purely formal axiomatic theory, as formal stipulations with definitional character. This raised two questions: 1) what relations can purely formal and conceptual theories entertain? 2) Are purely symbolic theories *in themselves* providers of knowledge of some sort?

The Göttingen lectures contain Husserl's fully articulated answer to question 1); In *LI* he answers 2): purely symbolic systems, provided they are consistent, give us formal knowledge; formal theories (which is a part of formal logic – the theory of formal manifolds and formal theories) constitute the most general investigation of the *forms* under which we can (in principle) experience objects in general. Husserl treatment of symbolic knowledge in mathematics is then a coherent system of thought that was already under elaboration as soon as 1890 and was in its main lines clearly sketched not after 1896 (although it may have suffered some influence, as for some metamathematical ideas – I have in mind the concept of completeness, in

---

[28] *Hua* XII, pp. 375-79: "The Concept of General Arithmetic", p. 378, 1890.
[29] *Hua*, XII, pp.380-84: "Arithmetic as an A Priori Science".
[30] *Hua* XII, pp. 385-407: "On Set Theory".

particular – from Hilbert's papers of 1899 and 1900 on the axiomatization of Euclidian geometry and the arithmetic of real numbers as purely symbolic systems – influences on the reverse direction are also, of course, likely).

Being contemporaneous with the publication of *LI*, however, the Göttingen talks cannot be expected to be completely silent about the second problem. In fact, the idea of mathematics in the highest sense as the theory of *purely formal* mathematical system, which Husserl fully-developed conception of logic allocates within the third level of formal logic, is clearly presented and defended: "in the highest and most general sense mathematics is the science of theoretical systems in general, abstracting the objects of theoretical interest of given theories of different sciences; in no matter which given theory, in no matter which given deductive system, we abstract its subject matter, the particular types of objects it tried to theoretically master, and if we substitute the representations of objects materially determinate by simple formulas, that is, the representation of objects in general that is mastered by such a theory by a theory of this form, we have then accomplished a generalization that considers the given theories as particular cases of a class of theories, or rather of a form of theory that we consider in a unifying manner and in virtue of which we can say that all these particular scientific domains have, as form is concerned, the same theory."[31] "Mathematics is then, according to its highest ideal, a doctrine of theories, the most general science of deductive systems that are possible in general."[32]

The answers Husserl provided for the problem of symbolic knowledge, taken together, constitute Husserl's largely successful attempt to give formal mathematics, in all its variants, a completely satisfactory epistemological justification.

I believe I have already made clear the role the problem of symbolic knowledge, and Husserl's treatment of it, played in the development of his philosophy. Some people, however, are sometimes puzzled by the fact that Husserl, despite his emphasis on intuitions as the substance of knowledge – a point of view central to his philosophy from *LI* on, but already present in earlier works – never doubted the possibility of obtaining knowledge by purely symbolic means. Contrary to what some recent lectures of Husserl influenced by intuitionism may lead us to believe, Husserl's philosophy of mathematics emphasizes the epistemic relevance of symbolic mathematics, which is not seen as a meaningless symbolic "game", but real knowledge. Is this philosophy consistent? Shouldn't Husserl's claim that knowledge

---

[31] *Hua* XII, pp. 430-451: "The Imaginary in Mathematics", pp. 430-31.
[32] Id. ib. p. 432. This shows, in particular, that Husserl was not, in the Göttingen talks, aiming to disqualify *tout court* general arithmetic, and other purely symbolic systems, as providers of knowledge; or only justifying them as practical but essentially dispensable tools (in contrast with the views of *LI*). No, it was always clear to him that formal mathematics is a form of knowledge, knowledge of logical forms precisely; only the *problem* investigated in Göttingen was a a different one: what role *purely formal* theories can *justifiably* play when *conceptual* knowledge is at stake?

requires the fulfillment of empty intentions with proper intuitions disqualify symbolic mathematics as a provider of knowledge, of no matter which sort?

Of course, the answer to this question, as I believe to have shown, is no.

The problem of symbolic knowledge, however, opened up a plethora of difficult questions concerning knowledge, the role of intuition vis-à-vis intuitively empty representations and other epistemological problems that required a fresh philosophical start. It was the beginning of phenomenology.

Husserl himself says so: "Above all it was its [arithmetic's, *JJS*] *purely symbolic* [my emphasis] procedural techniques, in which the genuine, original insightful sense seemed to be interrupted and made absurd under the label of the transition trough the 'imaginary', that directed my thoughts to the significance and to the purely linguistic aspects of the thinking – and *knowing* [my emphasis] – processes and from that point on forced me to general 'investigations' which concerned universal clarification of the sense, the proper delimitation, and the unique accomplishment of formal logic" (*Draft Introduction to 'Logical Investigations'*. Hua 20/1: 272-329, p. 294, n.3. *Apud*, Moran **2005,** p.90)

The view that symbolic manipulations are a sort of game with letters, however, Husserl could not accept. For, how, he asks, can such a game have *scientific* applications? Symbolic knowledge is, in its highest expression, formal knowledge; but, he insists, when a given conceptually circumscribed domain is concerned, any given formal theory that is not equiform with the theory of this domain can only be epistemologically relevant for our knowledge of the domain in question under the restrictive conditions stated above. More or less the same sort of considerations appears in *Crisis*. In this book, his last (written in 1935-38, but published posthumously), Husserl detected a crisis of modernity characterized by an ingenuous but uncritical use of formal mathematical methods in science, whose seeds, according to him, were sown by the very creators of modern science, Galileo in particular. I do not want to go into a detailed analysis of these claims here; it suffices to notice, in order to appreciate the importance of the problem of symbolic knowledge in Husserl's philosophy, that the way he pointed out for modernity to overcome its "formalist alienation" was to go back to the *Lebenswelt* from where he thought scientific methods derive their sense (the scientist should always be able to recover the forgotten sense of the formal methods he utilizes). This recipe bear witness to Husserl's constant preoccupation to keep symbolic methods in science and mathematics far from degenerating into a pure and epistemologically unjustified game with signs.

References

da Silva, J. 2000a. "Husserl's Two Notions of Completeness". *Synthese* 125, pp. 417-38.

_____. 2000b. "Husserl's Conception of Logic". *Manuscrito* 22, pp. 367-397.

_____. 2000c. "The Many Senses of Completeness". *Manuscrito* 23, pp. 41-60.

_____. 2010. "Beyond Leibniz: Husserl' Vindication of Symbolic Knowledge". In M. Hartimo (ed.) *Phenomenology and Mathematics*, Springer, pp. 123-145.

FØllesdal, D. 1958. "Husserl and Frege: A Contribution to Elucidating the Origins of Phenomenological Philosophy". In Haaparanta (ed.) pp. 3-47. Translation of his Norwegian Master's Thesis.

Haaparanta, L. (ed.). 1994. *Mind, Meaning and Mathematics, Essays on the Philosophical Views of Husserl and Frege.* Dordrecht: Kluwer.

Hilbert, D. 1971. *Foundations of Geometry.* Engl. trans. of *Grundlagen der Geometrie*, 10th ed. (trans. L. Unger). La Salle, Ill.: Open Court.

Hintikka, J. (ed.). 1995. *From Dedekind to Gödel, Essays on the Development of the Foundations of Mathematics.* Dordrecht: Kluwer.

Husserl, E. 1970. *Philosophie der Arithmetik*: *Mit ergänzenden Texten (1890 – 1901)*, ed. L. Eley. *Husserliana*, vol. XII. The Hague: M. Nijhoff.

_____. 1979. *Husserliana*, vol. XXII. The Hague: M. Nijhoff.

_____. 2001. *Logical Investigations* (trans. J. N. Findlay), 2 vols. London and New York: Routledge.

_____. 1983. *Studien zur Arithmetik und Geometrie, Texte aus dem Nachlass (1886-1901). Husserliana*, vol. XXI. The Hague: M. Hijhoff.

_____. 1983. *Ideas Pertaining to a Pure Phenomenology and to a Phenomenological Philosophy, First Book* (trans. F. Kersten). Dordrecht: Kluver.

_____. 1969. *Formal and Transcendental Logic* (trans. D. Cairns). The Hague: M. Nijhoof.

_____. 1970. *The Crisis of European Science and Transcendental Phenomenology* (trans. D. Carr). Evanston, Ill.: Northwestern University Press.

French J. (ed.). 1975. *Edmund Husserl: Articles sur la logique (1890-1913)*. Paris: PUF.

Majer, U. 1997. "Husserl and Hilbert on Completeness: A Neglected Chapter in Early Twentieth Century Foundations of Mathematics", *Synthese* 110, pp. 37-56.

Moran, D. 2005. *Edmund Husserl, Founder of Phenomenology*. Cambridge: Polity Press.

Ortiz Hill, C. 1991. *Word and Object in Husserl, Frege, and Husserl. The Roots of Twentieth-Century Philosophy*. Athens: Ohio University Press.

Ortiz Hill, C. 1995. "Husserl and Hilbert on Completeness". In Hintikka ed., pp. 143-63, reprinted in Ortiz Hill & Rosado Haddock 2000.

Ortiz Hill, C and Rosado Haddock, G. 2000. *Frege or Husserl? Meaning, Objectivity, and Mathematics*. Chicago: Open Court.

Seebohm, T.; FØllesdal, D and Mohanty, J. (ed.). 1991. *Phenomenology and the Formal Sciences*. Dordrecht: Kluwer.

Willard, D (ed.). 1994. *Edmund Husserl: Early Writings in the Philosophy of Logic and Mathematics*. Dordrecht: Kluwer.

www.ingramcontent.com/pod-product-compliance
Lightning Source LLC
Chambersburg PA
CBHW071331190426
43193CB00041B/1486